Cruising Through Research

CRUISING THROUGH RESEARCH
Library Skills for Young Adults

John D. Volkman

1998
Libraries Unlimited, Inc.
and Its Division
TEACHER IDEAS PRESS
Englewood, Colorado

This book is dedicated to my mother (a retired high-school librarian) and father, Elizabeth and Ernest Volkman, who have so lovingly supported me in this project and every other aspect of my life. They passed on to me their love of books and service to people. No one could have a better heritage. Also, I want to thank Becky Shiner, a science teacher at Hoover High School, who has encouraged and inspired me for years in making the library at Hoover and me the best we can be.

Copyright © 1998 John D. Volkman
All Rights Reserved
Printed in the United States of America

No part of this publication may be reproduced, stored in a retrieval system, or transmitted, in any form or by any means, electronic, mechanical, photocopying, recording, or otherwise, without the prior written permission of the publisher. An exception is made for individual librarians and educators, who may make copies of activity sheets for classroom use in a single school. Other portions of the book (up to 15 pages) may be copied for in-service programs or other educational programs in a single school or library. Standard citation information should appear on each page.

Libraries Unlimited, Inc.
and Its Division
TEACHER IDEAS PRESS
P.O. Box 6633
Englewood, CO 80155-6633
1-800-237-6124
www.lu.com

Production Editor: Kay Mariea
Copy Editor: Jan Krygier
Proofreader: Matt Stewart
Layout and Design: Pamela J. Getchell

Library of Congress Cataloging-in-Publication Data

Volkman, John D.
  Cruising through research : library skills for young adults / John D. Volkman.
    xv, 207 p. 22x28 cm.
  Includes bibliographical references.
  ISBN 1-56308-536-4
  1. Library orientation for high school students--United States.
I. Title.
Z711.2.V65   1998
025.5'678223--DC21   97-40408
                                                                             CIP

5 6 7 8 9 10

Contents

Acknowledgments ix
Introduction xi
    Before You Set Sail xiii

Excursion 1: Six Basic Reference Books 1
    Six Basic Reference Books Instructions 1
        Destination: Reference Readiness 1
        Cargo 1
        Preparation 2
        Mooring 2
        Bearings 2
        Navigating Through Reference Reef 2
        Crew's Special Orders 4
        Captain's Orders 4
        Drydock 5
    Six Basic Reference Books Bibliography 5
        Basic Reference Books 6
        Sample Questions 7
        Six Basic Reference Books 8
        Basic 6 Reference Questions 9
        Basic 6 Reference Answers 45

Excursion 2: English Reference Books 51
    English Reference Books Instructions 51
        Destination: English Reference Readiness 51
        Cargo 51
        Preparation 52
        Mooring 52
        Bearings 52
        Navigating Through Reference Reef 52
        Crew's Special Orders 53
        Captain's Orders 53
        Drydock 54
    English Reference Books Bibliography 54
        English Reference Books 56
        Sample Questions 57
        English Reference Books Annotated List 58
        English Reference Questions 61
        English Reference Answers 97

Excursion 3: Patriot Passage ... 107
Patriot Passage Instructions ... 107
- Destination: Term-Paper Tactics ... 107
- Cargo ... 107
- Preparation ... 108
- Navigation Instructions ... 108
- Automatic Pilot ... 110
- Drydock ... 111
- Additional Naval Stores ... 111

Patriot Passage Bibliography ... 111
- Port of Call ... 111
- Quotation ... 112
- Author ... 112
- Disease ... 112
- Animal ... 112
  - *Patriot Passage Authors* ... 113
  - *Patriot Passage II* ... 114
    - Your Future forms ... 116
    - Research Notes forms ... 117
  - *Sample Transparencies* ... 118

Excursion 4: Queen Elizabeth Cruise ... 129
Queen Elizabeth Instructions ... 129
- Destination: Term-Paper Tactics ... 129
- Cargo ... 129
- Preparation ... 130
- Navigation Instructions ... 130
- Automatic Pilot ... 133
- Drydock ... 133
- Additional Naval Stores ... 133

Queen Elizabeth Bibliography ... 133
- Author ... 133
- Port of Call ... 134
- Animal ... 134
- Home ... 134
- Quotation ... 134
- Famous Person ... 135
- Disease ... 135
  - *Queen Elizabeth Authors* ... 136
  - *Queen Elizabeth II* ... 137
    - Your Future forms ... 139
    - Research Notes forms ... 140
  - *Sample Transparencies* ... 141

Contents / vii

Excursion 5: **World War II** 159
    World War II—Biography Instructions 159
        World War II—Biography 160

Excursion 6: **Biography** 163
    Biography Letter 163
        Biography Letter Assignment Sheet 164
        Famous Authors 166
        Famous Persons 167

Excursion 7: **Expose a Word** 169
        Expose a Word Assignment Sheet 170
        Expose a Word Word List 172

Excursion 8: **Farewell to Manzanar** 173
        Ideas for Teachers Introducing This Unit 174
        Farewell to Manzanar Assignment Sheet 175

Excursion 9: **Endangered Species** 177
        Endangered Species Assignment Sheet 178

Excursion 10: Foreign Languages, Foreign Countries 181
        Latin American Countries Assignment Sheet 182
        Traveling in an Hispanic Country 184
        Biography of an Hispanic Person, Past or Present . . . 187
        Los Hispanos Famosos 189

Excursion 11: Astronomy 191
        Astronomy Project 192

Excursion 12: Vietnam 195
    Vietnam Instructions 195
        Station 1 196
        Station 2 196
        Station 3 196
        Station 4 197
        Station 5 197
        Station 6 197
    Teacher Directions for Vietnam Project 197
        Folders 197

Excursion 12: Vietnam (*continued*)

    Teacher Directions for Vietnam Project (*continued*)

        Stations 198
- *Vietnam Notebook Cover Sheet* 199
- *Station 1—Map Activity Sheet* 200
- *Station 2—Vietnam Topics* 202
- *Station 3—Vietnam Era Songs* 203
- *War Protest Songs* 205
- *Station 4—Vietnam Poetry* 206
- *Stations 5 and 6—Vietnam Editorial and Commentary, Letters Home Graphics* 207

Acknowledgments

Robert Skapura, formerly a high-school librarian and now the Director of Learning Resources at the college level, has been my mentor in developing reference questions and units for 20 years. It was he who originally made up reference questions in an Apple format called "Skills Maker" in 1984. His ideas and enthusiasm have long been inspirational to me. This book builds on his foundation.

Wanda Moore, an English teacher at Hoover High School in Fresno, California, gave me the idea for developing the cruise units in 1988. Our cruise unit was adapted from an article by Joseph W. Peacock entitled "Research Revisited; or How I Learned to Love the Reader's Guide" (*English Journal*, November 1987, copyright National Council of Teachers of English).

Being a Vietnam-era veteran, I most love to share with students the unit on Vietnam. Roberta Rohde, librarian at Clovis (California) West High School, deserves the credit for creating the major components of this unit, and I thank her for allowing me to use it and develop it further. Rick Lyons, Sandra Person, and Kathy Torosian, social studies teachers at Hoover High School, also helped me further develop this unit.

Indeed, library units are developed in cooperation with teachers. Thus I must acknowledge some of the teachers who helped me with these units. The World War II excursion started with a research paper assignment from Rick Lyons. The endangered species excursion started with Kathy Markovich, a language arts teacher, and Hal Froese, a science teacher. The foreign language excursion was developed in cooperation with Sharlene Dunbar, a foreign language teacher. The astronomy excursion came courtesy of Becky Shiner, a science teacher. Wanda Moore gave me the idea for the Expose a Word excursion. I am grateful to have the privilege of working with such talented, dedicated, caring, fun teachers. They are one of the main reasons I love to go to work every day.

Introduction

Term paper. Research. Note-taking. Somehow these words seem to have become dirty words to both teachers and students. When I first started as the librarian at Hoover High School in Fresno, California, I observed that few teachers assigned research papers or used the resources of the library. The teachers who did (senior government teachers) just assigned a term paper assuming that the students knew how to write one. The result was that the students were frustrated and the instructors were dismayed and decried the ignorance of their "seniors."

Considering this state of affairs, I realized that if the students were to learn how to do research and use the library, it would be up to me to lead the way. Many of the teachers had given up because of the hostile attitude of my predecessor and because they didn't know how to proceed.

As a history major in college and an avid reader, I, of course, love to do research and learn new things. I always felt that I learned more from term papers than from studying for tests because, with term papers, I had to digest the information, organize it, and then put it in my own words. My dad always told me, "You have to learn through your fingers" (by writing). Also, "Knowledge for knowledge's sake" does not seem irrelevant to me. However, today's students need other motivators: future use, fun, grades.

"Why do I need to know this? This is boring. Do we get points for this?"

Do these questions sound familiar? In developing lessons, I have tried to address these issues. The cruise assignments are basically term papers in disguise. It's a disguise that works because it makes the assignment "fun." The future relevance of using almanacs, *Current Biography*, and other reference tools in upcoming classes in high school and college and for one's own use is emphasized, as are the importance of note-taking skills and making a proper bibliography. It is also not a small accomplishment to practice thinking skills; employers want workers who can think for themselves when attacking a problem.

To teach research skills to my freshmen I begin by teaching them to use basic reference books. The "Basic Six" and the "English Reference Books" are taught not only as sources in themselves, but also as a method to familiarize students with indexes, reference-book formats, and alphabetization. It really is like a treasure hunt, and most students find it fun and challenging.

The cruise assignments are couched in terms of a letter; the students are encouraged to write informally and to get credit for writing (passing) a letter (note) to a classmate instead of getting into trouble for it. The reference books chosen for the students to use in constructing the paper have been selected because they are used by many other classes and students need to be familiar with them. Also, many students are fascinated by books like the wildlife and medical encyclopedias, and it is heartwarming to see them share interesting pictures and facts with their classmates as they do the research!

In planning research at your school, start with the teachers who show the most interest. Work with them and develop good units. Normally, other teachers who teach in the same discipline are more than glad to use a unit that has already been developed. Things have a way of mushrooming, so do not try to hook all the teachers the first year. Start small and watch the interest grow.

The development of the World War II biography lesson is a prime example of how a lesson evolves. In the second semester of my first year at Hoover High School, I noticed that all of our books on Adolf Hitler, Benito Mussolini, and Franklin Roosevelt were checked out. I soon discovered that the reason was that two U.S. history teachers had given the same assignment to all five of their classes: "Write a term paper on one of these three people. Go!" They had neither instructed students in how to do a term paper nor consulted with me. Consulting with me would have allowed us to decide the availability of sources, the feasibility of putting sources on reserve, which reference books would be helpful, and the need to bring the classes to the library for research. Needless to say, a lot of students were frustrated, and so was I.

Over the next couple of years we addressed some of these issues, but I remained frustrated because there were still too many students researching too few topics and not really knowing how to go about it.

Then a few years ago I attended a school library workshop and got the ideas I needed to make library research much more successful for the students and less frustrating for me. In fact, I went to the library the day after the workshop (Sunday) and completely rewrote the assignment because the teacher was going to give the assignment to the students the next week. The assignments in this book incorporate most of the principles enumerated in the "Before You Set Sail" section beginning on the next page and serve as models for other assignments.

Many of the handouts included in this book provide practical ideas that librarians can use immediately. Some librarians may want to adapt these lessons to fit their particular collections or localized needs. Beyond customizing lessons, though, this book provides formats that you can follow to construct your own units regardless of the discipline. That is really what I do as I work with different teachers: Follow a basic format and adapt it to fit their particular unit. As you read the book, you will quickly see what I mean.

The handouts can be easily changed and improved each year as the need arises. To make this procedure available to you, I have the copy for the handouts available for sale on computer disks. Please contact me for further information. For other information on this book, you can also contact the publisher, Libraries Unlimited.

John Volkman
8380 N. Raisina Ave.
Fresno, CA 93720

Before You Set Sail

To begin students' journeys in exploring good researching techniques, Excursions 1 and 2 provide a fun introduction to reference books, and Excursions 3 and 4 explore note-taking and basic organization of research papers. Once you have steered students through these waters, you are ready to act as travel agent and work with teachers to plan other, more specific excursions.

Almost any aspect of the curriculum offers countless opportunities to do library research. In Excursions 5 through 12, I present some of my favorite research units. Notice the similar formats used in the units and the importance of creating the units cooperatively with the teachers. In creating your own units, use the following plan as your navigational guide to smooth sailing.

Destination

To have the teacher and the librarian work together to create a successful learning experience for all students, the following guidelines are suggested:

1. Topics are carefully planned and reviewed by the teacher and librarian before they are assigned. If a topic is assigned to a student, the librarian and teacher should guarantee that resources are available.

2. Students are taught or are already familiar with the skills needed to find required information.

3. Students should have a clear understanding of the procedures for gathering, recording, and presenting their information.

4. Checkpoints are built in at various stages of the project to ensure that students are on task, on time, and receive help when necessary.

5. Days indicated may not be consecutive. Most times, two days in a row in the library is optimum. A third day depends on how well the class is utilizing its time. On some major research assignments it works well to give the students two days in the library and encourage them to do research on their own time for a couple of weeks. Then schedule one more library day shortly before the day the assignment is due.

Navigation Instructions

Day 1

1. After the assignment is handed out, the teacher goes over the various parts of it. The librarian will then briefly describe the sources and their locations.

xiv / Introduction

2. Find sources needed. Depending on the number of topics and sources, the librarian may pull the sources and put them on a library cart. If students pull the sources, they should be encouraged to leave them on a library cart for the next class or next day. Students copy or check them out (if enough sources are available to do so).

3. Students begin taking notes on "Research Notes" forms (see p. 117). Write notes in own words.

4. Teacher checks to be sure minimum number of sources and forms are completed.

Day 2 (and Day 3, if necessary)

1. Students continue to take notes and find additional sources, if necessary.

2. Teacher checks for minimum number of "Research Notes" forms, being sure bibliographic information is included on the forms.

Day 3 (or Day 4)

1. Students work on their rough drafts in class using just their notes.

2. Teacher checks rough drafts for minimum progress.

Day 4 (or Day 5)

1. Students finish rough drafts.

2. Teacher or students check the rough drafts.

3. Final draft may be completed at home or in class.

Cargo

Most research assignments will contain at least some aspects of the elements listed below. (Refer to Excursion 5 to see example with these elements in this order.)

Topic Line. The list of suggested topics is sometimes included on the bottom of the resource page or sometimes on a separate page. Other times, students may either draw topics out of a hat or choose them themselves on a first-come, first-served basis where the teacher keeps a master list of the topics chosen. The teacher and librarian can decide what works best for their assignment. Be sure the students write their selected topic at the top of their assignment sheet.

Due Date Line. Students should know from the beginning exactly when the assignment is due.

Assignment. Describe what kind of end product is expected—that is, whether it is a research paper, an oral report, or a graphic presentation. Also state the expected length either in pages or minutes. Be specific in detailing what kind of information is expected of the students. Students will do better reports if they know what is expected.

What Should Be Turned In. Let students know what they are required to turn in, both end products and research tools. The list below would be an example of what the teacher would expect:

1. Cover
2. Typed report
3. Research notes
4. Some kind of visual or graphic
5. Bibliography in proper format

Minimum Resource Requirements. Depending on the type of research being done, there are certain best sources or sources you want to be sure the students use. State which these are and if there is a minimum number of sources required.

Grading. From the points assigned, students will understand that not just the final product, but the research notes, visuals, and bibliography are all important parts of the assignment.

Resource Bibliography. This listing will include the most important reference sources to use (since they are often difficult to locate using just the computer card catalog), subjects to look up in the computer card catalog, general call numbers, and computer databases to use. It is not inclusive; there is no attempt to list all the books on the regular shelves. Instead, possible subject headings are listed so that students may have an idea of how to best search in the card catalog/computer. What I do try to make fairly complete is the list of reference books which might be helpful. There are many reference books that cannot be located using the card catalog/computer, or students might not think to look in such sources as *Current Biography* or reference books that cover the time period, such as *Great Events* or *America in the 20th Century*. Reference books are the heart of my library, so I want to make sure the students know which ones to use.

Excursion 1
Six Basic Reference Books

Six Basic Reference Books Instructions

Destination: Reference Readiness

Students will learn how to choose, find, and use six basic reference books that are not only important in their own right, but also show how reference books in general are used. Finding the answers to the questions is similar to going on a treasure hunt.

Cargo

Overhead projector
Overhead transparency marker
"Basic Reference Books" overhead (fig. 1.1 on p. 6; can be enlarged 25% when copied)
"Sample Questions" overhead (fig. 1.2 on p. 7)
36 "Basic 6 Reference Questions" sheets (six questions per sheet, one sheet per student)
"Basic Reference Books" handout (blue, laminated, a class set)
"Six Basic Reference Books" instructions handout (pink, laminated, five copies)
Two answer keys (one for librarian and one for teacher)
Red pen (for correcting question sheets)
Blue shelf labels
Two boxes (8 1/2" X 11" Xerox paper box lids work well)

Preparation

1. Make enough copies of the "Basic Reference Books" handout (fig. 1.1) so that each student has a copy. I suggest that you copy them on blue paper and laminate them so they last longer. Then provide each student with a different "Basic 6 Reference Questions" sheet. Make a transparency of the "Basic Reference Books" handout (fig 1.1) and of the "Sample Questions" (fig. 1.2). Use an overhead projector to make your presentation and a transparency marker to write on the "Sample Questions" transparency the abbreviation for each source as you explain it.

2. On your computer type out in large letters the names of the reference books being used. Copy these names on heavy blue paper. Use transparent book tape to attach these labels to the appropriate shelves where the six reference sets are located.

3. Make five copies of the "Six Basic Reference Books" instructions (fig. 1.3). I suggest that you copy them on pink paper and laminate them so they will last longer.

Mooring

It is preferable to give these instructions to students in the vicinity of the reference section so that you can point out the location of the books mentioned. Be sure to have the classroom teacher listen to the instructions and be available to help students as they do the lesson.

Bearings

In introducing the excursion, point out to the students that just as a ship's navigator must use the map appropriate to his destination, so too students need to use the right book to find the right answer. For example, you would not use a cookbook to look up a phone number or a phone book to look up a recipe. Additionally, you must look under the correct name or word once you have determined the proper book.

Navigating Through Reference Reef

1. Students will use six different reference books in answering their six questions. Each book is to be used only once, and each student will have different questions to ensure that they do their own work.

2. Explain that you will use your examples (which you are showing on the overhead projector) to explain to them how to find the answers to their questions. An effective technique I use to encourage the students to pay attention is to tell them that they will be limited to asking three questions following my presentation. Doing this helps eliminate the questions that the students can answer themselves but just want you to do for them. When a question like that is asked,

you can often respond with "Do you really want to use one of your questions on that?" Usually they will say "No." If you do answer a question, just put your initials in the upper right corner of the question sheet. Try it; it works!

3. Tell the students that the answers to the questions are usually found near the beginning of the article so that they do not have to read the whole article. Mention to the students that if they forget where the books are located, they can use the call numbers listed on the "Basic Reference Books" handout and then look for the blue strips.

4. Read the first sample question and ask "What kind of question is it?" It is about people because it contains a person's name and the question is asking about that person. Put an *X* in front of the word *Source* on your overhead sheet.

5. Do the same thing for questions 2 and 3. Then ask the students to find their three questions about people and put *X*s by them. Give them a few minutes to do this. Circulate to assist those who need help.

6. Once the three people questions are determined, the next step is to determine "Which Book?" To do this, we must ask additional questions. You and I, as librarians, do this automatically when we answer reference questions. Here, we are trying to model this process for students so that they can "think" their way to the right book by looking for the clues.

7. For the first question, ask "Is this person dead?" "Most likely, as he lived in the 1800s." "Is it probable that this person is an American?" "Yes, because he lived in Pennsylvania. So if this person is both dead and an American, there is a good chance he will be listed in the *Dictionary of American Biography*. An easy way to remember this is to think of it as *Dead American Biography*." Point out to the students where the set is located and then explain that the set consists of 10 volumes, arranged alphabetically by the person's last name. (The supplements are not used for this assignment.) "Look at your three people questions and pick out the *one* that is about a dead American. Write *DAB* as the source."

8. For the second question, ask "Is this person dead?" "No. Therefore, he cannot be found in *DAB*." "Has this person accomplished something since 1940 to make him famous?" "Yes. Then he could be listed in *Current Biography*." Show the students where the *Current Biography* is located. Explain that it describes important people worldwide and has been published once a year since 1940. "In order to find out in which annual edition a person is listed in *CB*, look in the cumulative index. Then go to that year and find the person listed alphabetically. Look at your remaining two people questions, choose the person who has accomplished something since 1940, and write *CB* as the source."

9. For the third question, ask "Is this person an American?" "No. Then she cannot be found in *DAB*. Has she accomplished something since 1940? No. Then she cannot be in *CB*. Our third reference book on people is the *McGraw-Hill Encyclopedia of World Biography*. Your

4 / Excursion 1: Six Basic Reference Books

third question concerns a dead non-American." Point out the encyclopedia and tell the students to "Keep in mind that *EWB* does include Americans and people who are alive, but for the sake of this lesson your person is a dead non-American. Write *EWB* as your source for the dead non-American."

10. For the fourth question again ask "What kind of a question is it?" "Because it is about a place, we'll look in the *Worldmark Encyclopedia of the Nations*." Point it out and mention "It is arranged by continent and then alphabetically by the name of the country. Choose your question about a country and write down *WEN* as the source."

11. For the fifth question again ask "What kind of a question is it?" "Since it relates to a statistic, we will use the *World Almanac*. Statistics-type questions include 'How much?' 'How high?' 'How long?' The *World Almanac* also lists current information which includes such examples as 'Who won the World Series, the Oscar, the Nobel Prize, etc.?' " Show the location of the almanacs and, turning to the index in one, point out "To use the almanac, you must refer to the index in the front of the book. Because the almanac is cumulative, you can find lists of all previous winners, not just the past year's winner. Write *WA* for your source on your question that asks for a statistic or current information."

12. For the last question, ask a final time "What kind of a question is it?" "Because it is about an event, we are going to look in the *Dictionary of American History*. Your last question should have something to do with American history. If it does, write down *DAH* as the source. If not, re-examine your questions to check your sources." Point out the location of the *Dictionary of American History* and indicate that it is alphabetical by the name of the event.

Crew's Special Orders

1. Before releasing the students to look up the answers, remind them to replace the books correctly on the shelves after they use them so the other students can find them.

2. Also, show them the two boxes you have set up on a table. They are to turn in their papers in these boxes at the end of the period, finished or not. They are to put their question sheets in one box and their blue laminated handouts in the other.

3. Then tell them to "Now go to the shelves and find the answers."

Captain's Orders

Correct the completed papers using the answer key. The next day, give back incomplete papers to be finished and have students who missed questions look again; after all, the purpose of this unit is for them to learn how to find the information correctly.

Drydock

Students who missed the presentation are given a sheet of six questions, the blue "Basic Reference Books" handout, and the pink "Six Basic Reference Books" instructions handout (fig. 1.3 on p. 8). Tell them to follow the directions on the pink handout exactly as they are written and that if they have specific questions as they go along to ask you as they occur.

Six Basic Reference Books Bibliography

(Editor's Note: Dates are not included on this list because of the many editions and the annual editions that exist for many reference books.)

Current Biography Yearbook. New York: H. W. Wilson.

Dictionary of American Biography. New York: Charles Scribner's Sons.

Dictionary of American History. New York: Charles Scribner's Sons.

The McGraw-Hill Encyclopedia of World Biography. New York: McGraw-Hill.

The World Almanac and Book of Facts. Mahwah, NJ: World Almanac Books.

Worldmark Encyclopedia of the Nations. Detroit: Gale Research.

Basic Reference Books

What Kind of a Question? Which Book?

About People	*Dictionary of American Biography*	**(DAB)**
	Current Biography	**(CB)**
	McGraw-Hill Encyclopedia of World Biography	**(EWB)**
About Places	*Worldmark Encyclopedia of the Nations*	**(WEN)**
About Statistics or Current Information	*World Almanac*	**(WA)**
About Events	*Dictionary of American History*	**(DAH)**

CURRENT BIOGRAPHY
Description: Covers important **contemporary** (since 1940) people in all fields. Includes a photograph of the person. Published yearly volume since 1940. Cumulative index covers 1940–1995.
Hint: Use the **index** to find the year **first**; each volume is arranged **alphabetically by last name**.

DICTIONARY OF AMERICAN BIOGRAPHY
Description: This comprehensive collection of short biographies of famous **dead Americans** covers people from 1776–1930 in the first 10 volumes, with 10 supplements to 1980.
Hint: Names are arranged **alphabetically by last name**. Refer to the cumulative index.

DICTIONARY OF AMERICAN HISTORY
Description: Short accounts of important **events** that have shaped America.
Hint: Entries are arranged **alphabetically by topic**; includes an index volume.

MCGRAW-HILL ENCYCLOPEDIA OF WORLD BIOGRAPHY
Description: Articles about people both **living and dead, American and non-American.** Includes a picture.
Hint: **Entries in the 12 volumes are arranged alphabetically by last name;** the index is in the last volume. Includes five supplements.

WORLD ALMANAC
Description: Contains information on just about any topic. Particularly useful for finding **statistics, lists, and current information.**
Hint: **Must use index** in front to find subject. Published **annually**.

WORLDMARK ENCYCLOPEDIA OF THE NATIONS
Description: Contains comprehensive descriptions of all **nations** in five volumes.
Hint: Volumes are arranged by **continent**, then **alphabetically by country**.

From *Cruising Through Research* © 1998 John D. Volkman. (800) 237-6124.

Fig. 1.1. Place your local call numbers to the left of each book. Make a copy for each student and laminate; make a transparency for use with the overhead projector.

Sample Questions

1. James Black was a lawyer in Pennsylvania in the mid 1800s. What party did he found?

   Source: _____
   Answer: _____
   _____

2. What university did basketball great Michael Jordan attend in the 1980s?

   Source: _____
   Answer: _____
   _____

3. English author Emily Brontë wrote *Wuthering Heights* in 1847. What were the names of her two sisters who were also authors?

   Source: _____
   Answer: _____
   _____

4. What is the chief export of the European country of Norway?

   Source: _____
   Answer: _____
   _____

5. What is the longest river in the world?

   Source: _____
   Answer: _____
   _____

6. In 1911, 147 people died in the Triangle Fire in New York. What did the Triangle Co. manufacture?

   Source: _____
   Answer: _____
   _____

From *Cruising Through Research* © 1998 John D. Volkman. (800) 237-6124.

Fig. 1.2. Sample Questions. Make a transparency.

Six Basic Reference Books

I. Each of your six questions will be answered from a different book. The six books are listed on the **blue sheet** that I have given you.

II. To answer those questions, you must first answer these three questions: What Kind of a Question? Which Book? Which Word?

III. Read the question and determine what kind of question it is, using the guidelines below:

   A. If it is a question about a person (look for a person's name), put an *X* by the word *Source*. Three of the questions on your question sheet will be about people.

   1. For the question that is about a dead American, use the *Dictionary of American Biography*. Write *DAB* for the source.

   2. For the question that is about someone who became famous since 1940, use *Current Biography*. Write *CB* for the source. (When you use *Current Biography*, you **must** use the index volume **first** to determine under which year you will be looking.)

   3. For the question that is about a dead, non-American, use the *McGraw-Hill Encyclopedia of World Biography*. Write *EWB* for the source.

   B. Of your remaining three questions, one is about a country. Use the *Worldmark Encyclopedia of the Nations* for this question and write *WEN* for the source.

   C. Look next for a question that asks about statistics or current information (How much? How tall? Who won the World Series, Oscar, etc?). Use the *World Almanac* to locate this kind of information. Write *WA* for the source. (When you use the almanac, refer to the index in the front of the book.)

   D. Your last question is about an event in American history. Use the *Dictionary of American History*. Write *DAH* for the source.

IV. Now go find the answers to the six questions using your six sources. The call number for each book is listed on the blue sheet, and there are blue labels on the reference shelves to help you find the reference books.

From *Cruising Through Research*. © 1998 John D. Volkman. (800) 237-6124.

Fig. 1.3. This page is given to students who were absent and missed the instructions given to the class.

Basic 6 Reference Questions

Name: _____

Teacher: _____ Period: _____

Sheet 1

1. What is the normal average temperature in San Francisco, California, in the month of January?

   Source: _____
   Answer: _____
   _____

2. In 1837, Laura Dewey Bridgman attended the Perkins Institution in Boston. How did she lose her sight and hearing, and how old was she?

   Source: _____
   Answer: _____
   _____

3. Belize is a little-known country in Central America. Which two ethnic groups make up the majority of its population?

   Source: _____
   Answer: _____
   _____

4. Dustin Hoffman won recognition in *The Graduate,* a late 1960s movie. What role did Hoffman play in a junior high school play? What was the name of the play?

   Source: _____
   Answer: _____
   _____

5. A notorious political scandal in the 1800s involved the Philadelphia Gas Ring, which charged high rates and gave no service. Name the group that defeated the ring.

   Source: _____
   Answer: _____
   _____

6. Robert Recorde is generally credited with introducing algebra to England in the early 1500s. What common algebraic sign is he credited with first using?

   Source: _____
   Answer: _____
   _____

From *Cruising Through Research.* © 1998 John D. Volkman. (800) 237-6124.

Basic 6 Reference Questions

Name: _____

Teacher: _____ Period: _____

Sheet 2

1. Many cities have underwater tunnels through which cars can drive. How long is the Detroit–Windsor tunnel, which passes under the Detroit River?

   Source: _____
   Answer: _____
   _____

2. When and where was the first Anti-Saloon League founded in the United States?

   Source: _____
   Answer: _____
   _____

3. Hugh Glass was a 19th-century trapper in the western United States who was left for dead by two men after he had been mauled by a bear. What were the names of the two men who left him for dead?

   Source: _____
   Answer: _____
   _____

4. Bob Dylan is a famous folk singer and composer who became well known in the late 1960s. His real name is Bob Zimmerman, but he changed it in honor of a famous poet whom he admired. Name the poet.

   Source: _____
   Answer: _____
   _____

5. The two major political parties in the United States are the Democrats and the Republicans. Name the two major parties in the tiny Asian country of Sri Lanka.

   Source: _____
   Answer: _____
   _____

6. Hatshepsut was a powerful queen who ruled ancient Egypt for many years. How long did she rule, and what happened to her name after she died?

   Source: _____
   Answer: _____
   _____

From *Cruising Through Research.* © 1998 John D. Volkman. (800) 237-6124.

Basic 6 Reference Questions

Name: _____

Teacher: _____ Period: _____

Sheet 3

1. Airlines often compute fares based on distances between cities. What is the airline mileage between Washington, D.C., and London?

   Source: _____
   Answer: _____
   _____

2. Midway Plaisance was an amusement center at the famous Chicago Exposition in the 1800s. Name the dance that "Little Egypt" did that so shocked people.

   Source: _____
   Answer: _____
   _____

3. Of what does the topography of Italy's mainland generally consist?

   Source: _____
   Answer: _____
   _____

4. John Glover was an American Revolutionary soldier. He helped build a hospital to treat what disease?

   Source: _____
   Answer: _____
   _____

5. Newspaper heiress Patricia Hearst was kidnapped in 1974. What was the name of the band of terrorists who took her?

   Source: _____
   Answer: _____
   _____

6. Edward Blyden was a Liberian educator and statesman in the 1800s. When he came to the United States to go to school, why was he not admitted?

   Source: _____
   Answer: _____
   _____

From *Cruising Through Research.* © 1998 John D. Volkman. (800) 237-6124.

Basic 6 Reference Questions

Name: _____

Teacher: _____ Period: _____

Sheet 4

1. Larry Csonka was a football player who became famous in the 1970s. What was his nickname?

   Source: _____
   Answer: _____
   _____

2. When did the first potatoes arrive in the United States? Along what river in the United States were they planted?

   Source: _____
   Answer: _____
   _____

3. Joel West Smith became prominent as an American educator of the blind in the early 1900s. How old was he when he became blind, and how did it happen?

   Source: _____
   Answer: _____
   _____

4. What is the ZIP code for Moss Point, Mississippi?

   Source: _____
   Answer: _____
   _____

5. What system of weights and measures is used in the African country of Chad?

   Source: _____
   Answer: _____
   _____

6. The Italian saint Francis founded the religious order called the Franciscans. What was his real first name given to him at birth?

   Source: _____
   Answer: _____
   _____

From *Cruising Through Research.* © 1998 John D. Volkman. (800) 237-6124.

Basic 6 Reference Questions

Name: _____

Teacher: _____ Period: _____

Sheet 5

1. *Rum Row* was a term used during Prohibition to describe the group of ships that brought illegal liquor into the United States. How far offshore did the "row" form?

    Source: _____
    Answer: _____
    _____

2. Which company spent the most money for advertising in any year after 1995?

    Source: _____
    Answer: _____
    _____

3. Adrian Anson was a professional baseball player when baseball was just beginning in the 1800s. In what years did he lead his Chicago team to a league championship?

    Source: _____
    Answer: _____
    _____

4. Mali is a small African country that was known as the Mali Empire in the 14th century. Who was the leader of the Mali Empire at that time?

    Source: _____
    Answer: _____
    _____

5. Roosevelt (Rosey) Grier became famous as a football player in the 1970s. He also served as a bodyguard for Robert F. Kennedy. What is the title of the book he wrote?

    Source: _____
    Answer: _____
    _____

6. Nichiren was a Japanese Buddhist monk in the 13th century. What does his name mean in English?

    Source: _____
    Answer: _____
    _____

From *Cruising Through Research.* © 1998 John D. Volkman. (800) 237-6124.

14 / Excursion 1: Six Basic Reference Books

Basic 6 Reference Questions

Name: _____

Teacher: _____ Period: _____

Sheet 6

1. Bill Cosby is noted as a comedian who gained national recognition in the mid 1960s. What was the name of the first television series in which he starred?

   Source: _____
   Answer: _____
   _____

2. What is the population of Grand Junction, Colorado, for any year in the 1990s?

   Source: _____
   Answer: _____
   _____

3. Sam Patch became famous in the 1800s in New Jersey as a daredevil diver, an occupation that eventually cost him his life. When he first started his career, he jumped from the Chasm Bridge into what river?

   Source: _____
   Answer: _____
   _____

4. Grenada became famous when U.S. troops invaded this Caribbean Island in 1983. What Grenada resource is pictured in the left-hand triangle of the Grenada flag?

   Source: _____
   Answer: _____
   _____

5. Schooner sailing vessels were widely used in the United States until the advent of steam-powered vessels in the mid-1800s. Where did the real schooner originate?

   Source: _____
   Answer: _____
   _____

6. The great Austrian composer Wolfgang Amadeus Mozart was born in 1756. By what age was he already a budding composer and accomplished keyboard performer?

   Source: _____
   Answer: _____
   _____

From *Cruising Through Research.* © 1998 John D. Volkman. (800) 237-6124.

Basic 6 Reference Questions

Name: _____

Teacher: _____ Period: _____

Sheet 7

1. Botswana is a small African country whose major tourist attraction is its wildlife. What is the major environmental problem facing Botswana today?

   Source: _____
   Answer: _____
   _____

2. When French novelist Jules Verne wrote *Around the World in 80 Days,* whom did he use to model the character of Phineas Fogg?

   Source: _____
   Answer: _____
   _____

3. Raymond Burr became famous in the 1960s for playing Perry Mason and then later Ironside. When he was only one year old, his family moved to another country and stayed for five years. Name the country.

   Source: _____
   Answer: _____
   _____

4. In the Sand Creek Massacre on November 29, 1864, Colorado militiamen killed about a third of a band of 500 Cheyenne Indians. Who was the chief of the Cheyenne?

   Source: _____
   Answer: _____
   _____

5. In the 1800s, William Blaikie was famous as an athlete and promoter of physical training in New York. When he was 17 years old he weighed 133 pounds. How much weight could he lift?

   Source: _____
   Answer: _____
   _____

6. On a calendar for the year 2000, on what day of the week will Christmas fall?

   Source: _____
   Answer: _____
   _____

From *Cruising Through Research.* © 1998 John D. Volkman. (800) 237-6124.

Basic 6 Reference Questions

Name: _____

Teacher: _____ Period: _____

Sheet 8

1. The Gunnison Massacre occurred in Utah in 1853. What group was charged with instigating the murders?

   Source: _____
   Answer: _____
   _____

2. What is the tallest building in Little Rock, Arkansas?

   Source: _____
   Answer: _____
   _____

3. Matthew Vassar founded Vassar College in Michigan in 1861. How did he make his money?

   Source: _____
   Answer: _____
   _____

4. Zimbabwe is an African country. What are its most serious environmental problems?

   Source: _____
   Answer: _____
   _____

5. Rafer Johnson was the 1960 Olympic decathlon champion. In what town near Fresno was he raised?

   Source: _____
   Answer: _____
   _____

6. Attila was a Hun chieftain who was known for pillaging and plundering in the 4th century. How did he die?

   Source: _____
   Answer: _____
   _____

From *Cruising Through Research*. © 1998 John D. Volkman. (800) 237-6124.

Basic 6 Reference Questions

Name: _____

Teacher: _____ Period: _____

Sheet 9

1. To what address would you send a fan letter if your favorite baseball team was the Boston Red Sox?

   Source: _____
   Answer: _____
   _____

2. The Sand Creek Massacre involved federal troops who killed about a third of a band of 500 Cheyenne Indians, many of them women and children. Who commanded the Colorado volunteers?

   Source: _____
   Answer: _____
   _____

3. The European country of Poland is mostly lowlands, but it does have one tall mountain. What is the name of it?

   Source: _____
   Answer: _____
   _____

4. Julio Roca was an Argentine general. How old was he when he first volunteered to fight?

   Source: _____
   Answer: _____
   _____

5. Actor Gregory Peck came to Hollywood in 1943. In what town was he reared?

   Source: _____
   Answer: _____
   _____

6. Seth Wyman was a thief all of his life from 1784 to 1843 in New Hampshire and Maine. What was the first thing he stole?

   Source: _____
   Answer: _____
   _____

From *Cruising Through Research.* © 1998 John D. Volkman. (800) 237-6124.

Basic 6 Reference Questions

Name: _____

Teacher: _____ Period: _____

Sheet 10

1. What is the all-time top television program, according to the Nielsen ratings?

   Source: _____
   Answer: _____
   _____

2. Joseph A. Slade, who lived in the 1800s, was a good man when sober and a very bad man when drunk. What did he do to "Old Jules" Reni after he shot him in Colorado?

   Source: _____
   Answer: _____
   _____

3. Herschel Walker won the Heisman trophy in 1982. How many NCAA records did he break while playing football at the University of Georgia?

   Source: _____
   Answer: _____
   _____

4. At what time in American history did the term *Shinplasters* originate?

   Source: _____
   Answer: _____
   _____

5. What mountains form the backbone of the European country of Romania?

   Source: _____
   Answer: _____
   _____

6. The Jewish poet Nelly Sachs published her first collection in 1921. At what age did she begin to write poetry?

   Source: _____
   Answer: _____
   _____

From *Cruising Through Research.* © 1998 John D. Volkman. (800) 237-6124.

Basic 6 Reference Questions

Name: _____

Teacher: _____ Period: _____

Sheet 11

1. How many languages are spoken in the African country of Zaire?

   Source: _____
   Answer: _____
   _____

2. Actor Ben Kingsley won an Oscar in 1982 for his performance in the movie *Gandhi*. His professional name is partially derived from what nickname?

   Source: _____
   Answer: _____
   _____

3. The tallest building in the world is in Chicago. What is the name of it?

   Source: _____
   Answer: _____
   _____

4. William A. A. Wallace was a Texas Ranger in the 1800s known for his bravery. Between what two cities did he contract to carry the mail? How far is that?

   Source: _____
   Answer: _____
   _____

5. The Salt War in Texas in 1877 developed into a feud between two men. Who were these two men?

   Source: _____
   Answer: _____
   _____

6. The Japanese politician Kei Hara went to Tokyo in 1872. What newspaper did he join at age 24?

   Source: _____
   Answer: _____
   _____

From *Cruising Through Research.* © 1998 John D. Volkman. (800) 237-6124.

20 / Excursion 1: Six Basic Reference Books

Basic 6 Reference Questions

Name: _____

Teacher: _____ Period: _____

Sheet 12

1. By what means did the first extensive public gambling in the United States take place?

   Source: _____
   Answer: _____
   _____

2. What language is spoken in the Asian country of Jordan?

   Source: _____
   Answer: _____
   _____

3. Dan Rice ran for the presidency in 1868. At the time, he was making $1,000 a week and was as well known as P. T. Barnum. What was his occupation?

   Source: _____
   Answer: _____
   _____

4. Sonny and Cher became famous in the 1970s. Some people know that Cher is part Cherokee. What other nationalities are in her family background?

   Source: _____
   Answer: _____
   _____

5. The French painter Paul Cezanne helped develop modern painting. In 1852, with whom did he form a friendship?

   Source: _____
   Answer: _____
   _____

6. In men's track and field, who won the gold medal in the 100-meter in the 1988 Olympics?

   Source: _____
   Answer: _____
   _____

From *Cruising Through Research.* © 1998 John D. Volkman. (800) 237-6124.

Basic 6 Reference Questions

Name: _____

Teacher: _____ Period: _____

Sheet 13

1. Who won the Nobel Prize in Chemistry in 1974? From what country was he?

   Source: _____
   Answer: _____
   _____

2. In 1968, North Korea captured a U.S. Navy ship, the *Pueblo*, believing it to be a spy ship. How many crewmen were seized?

   Source: _____
   Answer: _____
   _____

3. Jacob Crowninshield was a famous sea captain and merchant who, in 1796, brought to New York an animal never seen before by Americans. Name the animal.

   Source: _____
   Answer: _____
   _____

4. Mali is a landlocked country in West Africa. What is the major environmental problem facing Mali today?

   Source: _____
   Answer: _____
   _____

5. James Garner starred in a popular TV series called *The Rockford Files* in the 1960s. What was his real last name and how old was he when his mother died?

   Source: _____
   Answer: _____
   _____

6. Democritus was an ancient Greek philosopher. What theory did he promulgate?

   Source: _____
   Answer: _____
   _____

From *Cruising Through Research.* © 1998 John D. Volkman. (800) 237-6124.

Basic 6 Reference Questions

Name: _____

Teacher: _____ Period: _____

Sheet 14

1. Henry Winkler gained fame in the 1970s as "The Fonz." As a boy, in what two cities did he attend school?

    Source: _____
    Answer: _____
    _____

2. What is the tallest building in Birmingham, Alabama?

    Source: _____
    Answer: _____
    _____

3. The Yazoo Land Fraud was a land swindle in which the entire states of Alabama and Mississippi were illegally sold. At what price per acre were they sold?

    Source: _____
    Answer: _____
    _____

4. The European country of Romania was once part of the Roman Empire. Which Roman emperor conquered it and when?

    Source: _____
    Answer: _____
    _____

5. Raoul Gervais Victor Lufbery was perhaps the greatest American aviator in the First World War. How did he die?

    Source: _____
    Answer: _____
    _____

6. Matteo Ricci was an Italian Jesuit missionary around the year 1600. Why did he go to Rome in 1568?

    Source: _____
    Answer: _____
    _____

From *Cruising Through Research.* © 1998 John D. Volkman. (800) 237-6124.

Basic 6 Reference Questions

Name: _____

Teacher: _____ Period: _____

Sheet 15

1. Actress Jodie Foster, who starred in the 1991 film *Silence of the Lambs*, was also a child star. By what age did she have three of her films screened at the Cannes Film Festival?

    Source: _____
    Answer: _____
    _____

2. The Students for a Democratic Society (SDS) led protest movements in the 1960s and numbered 60,000 members. Who helped publish its "Port Huron Statement"?

    Source: _____
    Answer: _____
    _____

3. Andorra is a very small country in Europe. Most Andorran houses are made of the same building material. What is it?

    Source: _____
    Answer: _____
    _____

4. The second highest mountain in the world is in Asia. Name this mountain.

    Source: _____
    Answer: _____
    _____

5. Henry Plummer was a bandit in the 1800s. Why did he murder a man while he was marshal in Nevada City?

    Source: _____
    Answer: _____
    _____

6. Melaine Klein was an Austrian psychologist. In 1920, she was one of the first to engage in what kind of analysis?

    Source: _____
    Answer: _____
    _____

From *Cruising Through Research.* © 1998 John D. Volkman. (800) 237-6124.

Basic 6 Reference Questions

Name: _____

Teacher: _____ Period: _____

Sheet 16

1. In the "Panay Incident," Japanese bombers sank the gunboat *Panay* and three other U.S. ships. When did this incident occur?

   Source: _____
   Answer: _____
   _____

2. What does the topography of the Asian country of Kuwait consist almost entirely of?

   Source: _____
   Answer: _____
   _____

3. Joe Namath made a name for himself in the 1960s as a professional football player. When he first signed a contract with the Jets, how much money did he get, and what did he get as a fringe benefit?

   Source: _____
   Answer: _____
   _____

4. Charles A. Siringo was a cowboy, a detective, and a writer in the late 1800s. What was the title of the first book he wrote?

   Source: _____
   Answer: _____
   _____

5. How many people attend Buddhist churches in the United States?

   Source: _____
   Answer: _____
   _____

6. Louis Blanc was a French socialist in the 1800s. What ruined his father financially?

   Source: _____
   Answer: _____
   _____

From *Cruising Through Research.* © 1998 John D. Volkman. (800) 237-6124.

Basic 6 Reference Questions

Name: _____

Teacher: _____ Period: _____

Sheet 17

1. Mario Cuomo was governor of New York during the 1980s. Which Republican did he defeat to gain office?

   Source: _____
   Answer: _____
   _____

2. The Asian country of Nauru is the world's smallest independent country. The Nauruan flag has a 12-pointed white star on it. What does the star represent?

   Source: _____
   Answer: _____
   _____

3. Walter Wellman was a famous explorer who set a record for flying a blimp 1,008 miles in 1911. What famous discovery did he claim to make in the Bahamas?

   Source: _____
   Answer: _____
   _____

4. How many American soldiers died in battle in World War II?

   Source: _____
   Answer: _____
   _____

5. The "Pentagon Papers" was a study of American involvement in Vietnam. It caused an uproar when secretly copied and published in what newspaper in 1971?

   Source: _____
   Answer: _____
   _____

6. The early 20th-century Russian painter Chaim Soutine was born into a large family. How many children were there?

   Source: _____
   Answer: _____
   _____

From *Cruising Through Research*. © 1998 John D. Volkman. (800) 237-6124.

Basic 6 Reference Questions

Name: _____

Teacher: _____ Period: _____

Sheet 18

1. The Tonkin Gulf incident marked the beginning of the Vietnam War for the United States. Name the ship the United States said was attacked by the North Vietnamese.

   Source: _____
   Answer: _____
   _____

2. What is the address of the Aaron Burr Association?

   Source: _____
   Answer: _____
   _____

3. Because of its large population and shortage of arable land, Egypt has many environmental problems. What birds can be legally hunted?

   Source: _____
   Answer: _____
   _____

4. Victor Chapman was one of the first American pilots killed during the First World War. He was shot down over Verdun. When shot down, what was he carrying for a friend who was in a hospital?

   Source: _____
   Answer: _____
   _____

5. What happened to Irish poet Patrick Pearse after he led the 1916 Easter Rising against the British?

   Source: _____
   Answer: _____
   _____

6. Actress Daryl Hannah stared as a mermaid in the 1984 romantic hit comedy *Splash*. In what city was she born?

   Source: _____
   Answer: _____
   _____

From *Cruising Through Research*. © 1998 John D. Volkman. (800) 237-6124.

Basic 6 Reference Questions

Name: _____

Teacher: _____ Period: _____

Sheet 19

1. What daily newspaper has the largest circulation in the United States?

    Source: _____
    Answer: _____
    _____

2. What city in the European country of Greece has the environmental problem of industrial smog?

    Source: _____
    Answer: _____
    _____

3. Sue Grafton wrote the first of her series of detective novels in 1982. What is the name of the private investigator in this series?

    Source: _____
    Answer: _____
    _____

4. Who was commanding the National Guard in 1970 at Kent State University (Ohio) when the Guard panicked and shot a number of demonstrating students?

    Source: _____
    Answer: _____
    _____

5. Adam Forepaugh ran a circus for 26 years in the 1800s. He was so successful that his gate receipts averaged a quarter of a million dollars a year at times. From age 9 until age 20, he worked in his father's shop. What kind of a shop was it?

    Source: _____
    Answer: _____
    _____

6. Michael Ney was one of Napoleon's generals. His marriage was the handiwork of whom?

    Source: _____
    Answer: _____
    _____

From *Cruising Through Research*. © 1998 John D. Volkman. (800) 237-6124.

Basic 6 Reference Questions

Name: _____

Teacher: _____ Period: _____

Sheet 20

1. James Frederick Joy was a lawyer in Michigan and Illinois. He hired a young lawyer in the mid-1800s who would later become president. Name the president.

   Source: _____
   Answer: _____
   _____

2. How many miles of coastline does the United States have?

   Source: _____
   Answer: _____
   _____

3. "Tippecanoe and Tyler, Too!" was the presidential campaign slogan of the Whig party in the 1800s. Name the two candidates.

   Source: _____
   Answer: _____
   _____

4. George Lucas first became famous in the 1970s for his movie *Star Wars*. What was the name of his first feature film?

   Source: _____
   Answer: _____
   _____

5. The Asian country of Fiji is located in the South Pacific. What topographical feature surrounds these islands?

   Source: _____
   Answer: _____
   _____

6. The Dutch painter Jan Vermeer created only a small number of works in the mid-1600s. How many authentic works did he leave when he died?

   Source: _____
   Answer: _____
   _____

From *Cruising Through Research*. © 1998 John D. Volkman. (800) 237-6124.

Basic 6 Reference Questions

Name: _____

Teacher: _____ Period: _____

Sheet 21

1. In 1837, American Charles Tiffany opened a stationery and notion shop that later became an expensive jewelry store. How much money did he make in the first three days?

   Source: _____
   Answer: _____
   _____

2. By law, how old must you be to get married in the state of Alabama if you have your parents' permission? Give the specified ages for both the boy and the girl.

   Source: _____
   Answer: _____
   _____

3. Basketball player Earvin ("Magic") Johnson won the NCAA championship as a sophomore at what university?

   Source: _____
   Answer: _____
   _____

4. Andersonville was a Confederate prison during the Civil War. What did the prisoners' rations consist of?

   Source: _____
   Answer: _____
   _____

5. In the African country of Morocco, 99 percent of the people are of the same religion. What are they?

   Source: _____
   Answer: _____
   _____

6. The French engineer Alexandre-Gustave Eiffel not only designed the Eiffel Tower in Paris but also a number of bridges. What is his most famous bridge?

   Source: _____
   Answer: _____
   _____

From *Cruising Through Research.* © 1998 John D. Volkman. (800) 237-6124.

Basic 6 Reference Questions

Name: _____

Teacher: _____ Period: _____

Sheet 22

1. The Asian country of Cyprus has a mountain system called the Troodos Massif. What is the name of its highest point?

    Source: _____
    Answer: _____
    _____

2. Why did early American settlers erect tide mills?

    Source: _____
    Answer: _____
    _____

3. Name the horse that won the Kentucky Derby in 1980.

    Source: _____
    Answer: _____
    _____

4. Before Hugh Glass became famous as an early American trapper, he was forced to be a pirate. Who was the pirate who took Glass as a prisoner?

    Source: _____
    Answer: _____
    _____

5. John Hurt is a British actor who starred in *The Elephant Man* in the early 1980s. In his youth, what kind of roles did he usually get in his school plays?

    Source: _____
    Answer: _____
    _____

6. The German author Theodor Fontane was a correspondent during the Franco-Prussian War. For what reason was he was captured and almost executed?

    Source: _____
    Answer: _____
    _____

From *Cruising Through Research.* © 1998 John D. Volkman. (800) 237-6124.

Basic 6 Reference Questions

Name: _____

Teacher: _____ Period: _____

Sheet 23

1. Simon Girty was known as "the Great Renegade" because of his extreme cruelty when fighting the British and the American Indians. How did his father die?

   Source: _____
   Answer: _____
   _____

2. In the early 1980s, actress Beth Henley won a Pulitzer Prize for the first full-length play she ever wrote. What was the title of the play?

   Source: _____
   Answer: _____
   _____

3. Indoor bathtubs were not common until the middle of the 1800s. In what year was the first bathtub installed in the White House and who was president then?

   Source: _____
   Answer: _____
   _____

4. Ethiopia has more than 70 separate ethnic groups in its population. One of these groups consists of "Black Jews." What is the official name of this group?

   Source: _____
   Answer: _____
   _____

5. Auguste Rodin was born in Paris in 1840. Before he became a famous sculptor, he was rejected by the Ecole des Beaux-Arts. How many times was he rejected?

   Source: _____
   Answer: _____
   _____

6. On a calendar for the year 2001, on what day of the week will Christmas fall?

   Source: _____
   Answer: _____
   _____

From *Cruising Through Research.* © 1998 John D. Volkman. (800) 237-6124.

Basic 6 Reference Questions

Name: _____

Teacher: _____ Period: _____

Sheet 24

1. What is the most serious environmental problem facing the African nation of Gambia?

   Source: _____
   Answer: _____
   _____

2. Cholera first struck North America in 1832. New York lost more than 3,000 people in two months. Only two major American cities escaped the epidemic. Name them.

   Source: _____
   Answer: _____
   _____

3. Cheryl Tiegs modeled for 79 magazine covers in a three-year period in her early career. What was her salary range for one week's work?

   Source: _____
   Answer: _____
   _____

4. Stephen Quackenbush was an American naval officer during the Mexican War in the 1800s. Both the name of his hometown and the name of his ship were the same. What was it?

   Source: _____
   Answer: _____
   _____

5. The U.S. Open Golf Tournament began in 1900 for men and in 1948 for women. Name the men's and women's winners for 1980.

   Source: _____
   Answer: _____
   _____

6. In the 19th century, the English astronomer Sir William Huggins forged a new branch of science. What was it called?

   Source: _____
   Answer: _____
   _____

From *Cruising Through Research.* © 1998 John D. Volkman. (800) 237-6124.

Basic 6 Reference Questions

Name: _____

Teacher: _____ Period: _____

Sheet 25

1. What is the name of the world's highest dam?

   Source: _____
   Answer: _____
   _____

2. Baseball player Reggie Jackson starred for both the Oakland A's and New York Yankees. What American League award did he receive in 1973?

   Source: _____
   Answer: _____
   _____

3. Inez Boissevain was active in the American suffrage movement in the early 1900s. What was her nickname after she led a colorful demonstration mounted on a white horse?

   Source: _____
   Answer: _____
   _____

4. The term *Manifest Destiny* referred to the United States's continued territorial expansion. Where did this phrase first occur?

   Source: _____
   Answer: _____
   _____

5. The principal island of Japan contains the city of Tokyo. What is the name of that island?

   Source: _____
   Answer: _____
   _____

6. The German composer Richard Wagner was the most important figure in 19th-century music. Who was his idol?

   Source: _____
   Answer: _____
   _____

From *Cruising Through Research.* © 1998 John D. Volkman. (800) 237-6124.

Basic 6 Reference Questions

Name: _____

Teacher: _____ Period: _____

Sheet 26

1. The Republic of Panama in Central America is slightly smaller than what state in the United States?

   Source: _____
   Answer: _____
   _____

2. The *Liberator* was an antislavery newspaper published in Boston from 1831 to 1865. Who was its publisher?

   Source: _____
   Answer: _____
   _____

3. What breed has the most dogs registered with the American Kennel Club?

   Source: _____
   Answer: _____
   _____

4. Pauline Cushman was known as "the spy of the Cumberland" during the Civil War. When and how did she die?

   Source: _____
   Answer: _____
   _____

5. Jessica Lange received an Academy Award in 1982 for best supporting actress in *Tootsie*. What movie was she obsessed with as a child?

   Source: _____
   Answer: _____
   _____

6. Edgar Degas was a French impressionist painter in the late 1800s. What did he love from an early age?

   Source: _____
   Answer: _____
   _____

From *Cruising Through Research.* © 1998 John D. Volkman. (800) 237-6124.

Basic 6 Reference Questions

Name: _____

Teacher: _____ Period: _____

Sheet 27

1. Kim Novak starred in three movies in 1956. What were they?

   Source: _____
   Answer: _____
   _____

2. Robert Herrick was an English poet and Anglican parson in the 1600s. How many years did he live?

   Source: _____
   Answer: _____
   _____

3. The Battle of Fredericksburg was the scene of a decisive southern victory in the Civil War. The main battle was fought at the base of what heights?

   Source: _____
   Answer: _____
   _____

4. How many volumes (books) are in the Los Angeles Public Library?

   Source: _____
   Answer: _____
   _____

5. Lee's Ferry, Arizona, was named after John Doyle Lee. In 1877, he was shot for his part in the Mountain Meadows Massacre. How many wives and children did he have?

   Source: _____
   Answer: _____
   _____

6. The African country of Burundi is unique because it has both the tallest and shortest ethnic groups in the world. What are the names of these two groups?

   Source: _____
   Answer: _____
   _____

From *Cruising Through Research*. © 1998 John D. Volkman. (800) 237-6124.

Basic 6 Reference Questions

Name: _____

Teacher: _____ Period: _____

Sheet 28

1. Douglas Haig commanded the British forces during World War I. Where did he serve his first army duty?

   Source: _____
   Answer: _____
   _____

2. William Gilpin was an Indian fighter whose adventurous life reached its climax when he served as the first territorial governor of what state?

   Source: _____
   Answer: _____
   _____

3. In the "Noddles Island Skirmish," some colonial Americans battled a British marine guard. How many British soldiers were killed?

   Source: _____
   Answer: _____
   _____

4. What are Guatemala's two main environmental problems?

   Source: _____
   Answer: _____
   _____

5. Author Maya Angelou read one of her poems at President Clinton's inauguration in 1992. Who gave her the first name of "Maya"?

   Source: _____
   Answer: _____
   _____

6. What is the name and depth (in feet) of the deepest point in the Pacific Ocean?

   Source: _____
   Answer: _____
   _____

From *Cruising Through Research.* © 1998 John D. Volkman. (800) 237-6124.

Basic 6 Reference Questions

Name: _____

Teacher: _____ Period: _____

Sheet 29

1. What book won the Newbery Medal for 1994?

   Source: _____
   Answer: _____
   _____

2. The Russian empress Catherine the Great ruled Russia from 1762 to 1796. What was the name of the Grand Duke she married at age 15?

   Source: _____
   Answer: _____
   _____

3. What kind of climate does the Asian country of Thailand have?

   Source: _____
   Answer: _____
   _____

4. In 1865, the Fenian Movement in the United States had 250,000 members who raised money and arms to send to the Irish Revolutionary Brotherhood. Name their leader.

   Source: _____
   Answer: _____
   _____

5. Canadian singer Anne Murray has had numerous hit records. What is the name of the 1970 hit that helped her achieve stardom?

   Source: _____
   Answer: _____
   _____

6. Although Abigail Adams referred to her once as "the queen of sluts," what important role did Patience Wright play during the Revolutionary War?

   Source: _____
   Answer: _____
   _____

From *Cruising Through Research*. © 1998 John D. Volkman. (800) 237-6124.

Basic 6 Reference Questions

Name: _____

Teacher: _____ Period: _____

Sheet 30

1. Ferdinand Lassalle was a German socialist leader in the mid-1800s. His father was a wealthy Jewish merchant involved in what kind of trade?

   Source: _____
   Answer: _____
   _____

2. How many bank failures were there in the United States in 1990?

   Source: _____
   Answer: _____
   _____

3. What award-winning novel did Toni Morrison write in 1977?

   Source: _____
   Answer: _____
   _____

4. James B. Colgate founded the New York Gold Exchange. Where did he go in 1841?

   Source: _____
   Answer: _____
   _____

5. The Gaines case, probably the longest court suit in U.S. history, took 23 years to settle. What city did Myra Clark sue in the case?

   Source: _____
   Answer: _____
   _____

6. Belize is a little-known country in Central America. What is its official language?

   Source: _____
   Answer: _____
   _____

From *Cruising Through Research*. © 1998 John D. Volkman. (800) 237-6124.

Basic 6 Reference Questions

Name: _____

Teacher: _____ Period: _____

Sheet 31

1. What is the normal average temperature in Fresno, California, in the month of January?

   Source: _____
   Answer: _____
   _____

2. Simon Girty was captured by Indians in 1759 and later committed atrocious acts of cruelty. What was his nickname?

   Source: _____
   Answer: _____
   _____

3. Senegal is situated in western Africa. What is the name of its largest ethnic group?

   Source: _____
   Answer: _____
   _____

4. Debbie Meyer set three Olympic swimming records in the 1968 Games. What childhood disability did she overcome?

   Source: _____
   Answer: _____
   _____

5. The Fort Hill letter was written in South Carolina in 1832. It was a definitive statement of whose nullification doctrine?

   Source: _____
   Answer: _____
   _____

6. Marco Polo spent 17 years traveling in China, beginning in 1271. What was the name of the Mongol prince who headed the realm?

   Source: _____
   Answer: _____
   _____

From *Cruising Through Research.* © 1998 John D. Volkman. (800) 237-6124.

Basic 6 Reference Questions

Name: _____

Teacher: _____ Period: _____

Sheet 32

1. Many cities have underwater tunnels through which cars may drive. How long is the Brooklyn–Battery tunnel, which passes under the East River?

   Source: _____
   Answer: _____
   _____

2. John Witherspoon was a signer of the Declaration of Independence. What was his profession?

   Source: _____
   Answer: _____
   _____

3. What three types of climates are found in France?

   Source: _____
   Answer: _____
   _____

4. In 1979, Curtis Sliwa, a high school dropout, founded a group of young crime fighters in New York City. What was the name of this group?

   Source: _____
   Answer: _____
   _____

5. The Martin-Tolliver feud began in Kentucky in 1884. How many years did it last?

   Source: _____
   Answer: _____
   _____

6. The Danish physicist Hans Oersted began the study of electromagnetism in the early 1800s. At what university did he begin his teaching career?

   Source: _____
   Answer: _____
   _____

From *Cruising Through Research.* © 1998 John D. Volkman. (800) 237-6124.

Basic 6 Reference Questions

Name: _____

Teacher: _____ Period: _____

Sheet 33

1. In millions of pounds, what was the production of lard in the United States in 1980?

   Source: _____
   Answer: _____
   _____

2. John Rawlins was Chief of Staff under General Grant during the Civil War. What did he join in 1849?

   Source: _____
   Answer: _____
   _____

3. There are at least how many distinct groups in the African country of Gabon?

   Source: _____
   Answer: _____
   _____

4. Len Deighton's first novel was published in 1962. What was the name of this spy thriller?

   Source: _____
   Answer: _____
   _____

5. The Oberlin Movement was an antislavery movement that began in Cincinnati in 1834. What was the name of the seminary at which it started?

   Source: _____
   Answer: _____
   _____

6. In the late 1800s the German Robert Koch helped to establish the bacterial causes of a number of infectious diseases. What was one of the first diseases that he studied?

   Source: _____
   Answer: _____
   _____

From *Cruising Through Research.* © 1998 John D. Volkman. (800) 237-6124.

42 / Excursion 1: Six Basic Reference Books

Basic 6 Reference Questions

Name: _____

Teacher: _____ Period: _____

Sheet 34

1. What is the ZIP code for Bisbee, Arizona?

   Source: _____
   Answer: _____
   _____

2. Turner Ashby was a Confederate soldier. What was the name of his father's home?

   Source: _____
   Answer: _____
   _____

3. More than 90 percent of the population of the European country of Monaco belongs to what religion?

   Source: _____
   Answer: _____
   _____

4. What city did Edward Koch become mayor of in 1978?

   Source: _____
   Answer: _____
   _____

5. During the Civil War, Quantrill's Raid was really a massacre in which more than 150 people died. Against what city did the raid occur?

   Source: _____
   Answer: _____
   _____

6. The Russian revolutionary Aleksandr Kerensky failed to establish democracy in Russia in 1917. What university did he attend?

   Source: _____
   Answer: _____
   _____

From *Cruising Through Research.* © 1998 John D. Volkman. (800) 237-6124.

Basic 6 Reference Questions

Name: _____

Teacher: _____ Period: _____

Sheet 35

1. Westmont is a college in California. What is its address (city and ZIP code)?

   Source: _____
   Answer: _____
   _____

2. The *Powhatan* Incident occurred just before the start of the Civil War. Who was the Secretary of State who ordered the warship *Powhatan* to Fort Pickens instead of Fort Sumter?

   Source: _____
   Answer: _____
   _____

3. The South American country of Peru has three topographical regions. What are they?

   Source: _____
   Answer: _____
   _____

4. Actress Liza Minnelli was nominated for an Oscar in 1969. At what age did she make an auspicious New York debut in *Best Foot Forward*?

   Source: _____
   Answer: _____
   _____

5. Watts Pye was raised in Minnesota in the late 1800s. He eventually became a missionary to what country?

   Source: _____
   Answer: _____
   _____

6. The English author Daniel Defoe published *Robinson Crusoe* in 1719. By then, he had been married 25 years. How many children did he have?

   Source: _____
   Answer: _____
   _____

From *Cruising Through Research.* © 1998 John D. Volkman. (800) 237-6124.

Basic 6 Reference Questions

Name: _____

Teacher: _____ Period: _____

Sheet 36

1. What is the population of Tuskegee, Alabama?

   Source: _____
   Answer: _____
   _____

2. John Colter was a trapper who helped Lewis and Clark explore Yellowstone in 1807. How much did his pack weigh?

   Source: _____
   Answer: _____
   _____

3. What is the climate near the coast of the Asian country of Pakistan?

   Source: _____
   Answer: _____
   _____

4. Robert Redford became famous in the 1970s as an actor. When he went to college to major in art, he was on a sports scholarship. For which sport?

   Source: _____
   Answer: _____
   _____

5. The Bay of Pigs invasion of Cuba on April 17, 1961, was a monumental failure for the Kennedy administration. What United States agency organized and financed the attempt?

   Source: _____
   Answer: _____
   _____

6. English admiral Horatio Nelson is noted for his victory at the Battle of Trafalgar. At what age did he enter the Royal Navy?

   Source: _____
   Answer: _____
   _____

From *Cruising Through Research.* © 1998 John D. Volkman. (800) 237-6124.

Basic 6 Reference Answers

SHEET 1
1. WA — 48 °F
2. DAB — She suffered an attack of scarlet fever when she was two and a half years old
3. WEN — Creole and Mestizo
4. CB 69 — Tiny Tim in *A Christmas Carol*
5. DAH — The Committee of One Hundred
6. EWB — Equal sign

SHEET 2
1. WA — 5,160 ft.
2. DAH — 1893 in Ohio
3. DAB — James Bridger and Fitzgerald
4. CB 65 — Dylan Thomas
5. WEN — Sri Lanka Free Party and United Nation Party
6. EWB — 20 years; her name was erased from all monuments

SHEET 3
1. WA — 3,674 miles
2. DAH — The hoochee-coochee
3. WEN — mountains
4. DAB — smallpox
5. CB 82 — The Symbionese Liberation Army (SLA)
6. EWB — Because of his race

SHEET 4
1. CB 77 — The lawn mower
2. DAH — 1621; along the James River
3. DAB — 24; during a Fourth of July accident
4. WA — 39567
5. WEN — Metric
6. EWB — Giovanni

SHEET 5
1. DAH — 3 miles
2. WA — Procter & Gamble
3. DAB — 1880, 1881, 1882, 1885, 1886
4. WEN — Mansa Musa
5. CB 75 — *The Rosey Grier Needlepoint Book for Men*
6. EWB — Sun lotus

SHEET 6
1. CB 67 — "I Spy"
2. WA — 29,255
3. DAB — Passaic
4. WEN — Nutmeg
5. DAH — Gloucester, Massachusetts
6. EWB — Age 6

From *Cruising Through Research*. © 1998 John D. Volkman. (800) 237-6124.

46 / Excursion 1: Six Basic Reference Books

SHEET 7
1. WEN — Overgrazing by cattle
2. EWB — His father
3. CB 61 — China
4. DAH — Black Kettle
5. DAB — 1,019 pounds
6. WA — Monday

SHEET 8
1. DAH — Mormons
2. WA — TCBY Towers
3. DAB — As a brewer and merchant
4. WEN — Erosion and deforestation
5. CB 61 — Kingsburg
6. EWB — From a hemorrhage due to excessive drinking

SHEET 9
1. WA — 24 Yawkey Way, Boston, MA 02215
2. DAH — Col. J. M. Chivington
3. WEN — Mount Rysy
4. EWB — 15 years old
5. CB 47 — La Jolla, California
6. DAB — A silver dollar

SHEET 10
1. WA — "M*A*S*H" special
2. DAB — He cut off his ears
3. CB 85 — 10
4. DAH — The American Revolution
5. WEN — The Carpathian Mountains
6. EWB — Age 17

SHEET 11
1. WEN — 700
2. CB 83 — Kingclove
3. WA — Sears Tower
4. DAB — San Antonio and El Paso; 600 miles
5. DAH — Louis Cardis and Charles Howard
6. EWB — *Hochi*

SHEET 12
1. DAH — Lottery
2. WEN — Arabic
3. DAB — A circus clown
4. CB 74 — Armenian, Turkish, French
5. EWB — Emile Zola
6. WA — Carl Lewis

From *Cruising Through Research.* © 1998 John D. Volkman. (800) 237-6124.

SHEET 13
1. WA   Paul J. Flory; United States
2. DAH   83
3. DAB   An elephant
4. WEN   Increasing desertification
5. CB 66 Bumgarner; five years old
6. EWB   Atomic theory

SHEET 14
1. CB 76 Lausanne, Switzerland and New York City
2. WA   Southtrust Tower
3. DAH   1.5 cents
4. WEN   Trajan; 106 A.D.
5. DAB   Jumping from his burning plane
6. EWB   To study law

SHEET 15
1. CB 81 Age 13
2. DAH   Tom Hayden and Al Haber
3. WEN   Stone
4. WA   K2 (Godwin Austen)
5. DAB   The man had had an intrigue with his wife
6. EWB   Child

SHEET 16
1. DAH   1937
2. WEN   Desert and mud flats
3. CB 66 $387,000 and a white Cadillac
4. DAB   *A Texas Cowboy, or Fifteen Years on the Hurricane Deck of a Spanish Pony*
5. WA   780,000 (1997)
6. EWB   The fall of the French empire

SHEET 17
1. CB 83 Lewis E. Lehrman
2. WEN   The original 12 tribes of Nauru
3. DAB   The place where Columbus first landed
4. WA   292,000
5. DAH   *New York Times*
6. EWB   11

SHEET 18
1. DAH   The *Maddox*
2. WA   4520 King Edward Ct., Annadale VA 22003
3. WEN   None
4. DAB   Some oranges
5. EWB   He was executed
6. CB 90 Chicago

From *Cruising Through Research.* © 1998 John D. Volkman. (800) 237-6124.

48 / Excursion 1: Six Basic Reference Books

SHEET 19
1. WA — *Wall Street Journal*
2. WEN — Athens
3. CB 47 — Kinsey Millhone
4. DAH — Robert Canterbury
5. DAB — A meat shop
6. EWB — Josephine Bonaparte

SHEET 20
1. DAB — Abraham Lincoln
2. WA — 12,383
3. DAH — William Henry Harrison and John Tyler
4. CB 78 — *THX 1138*
5. WEN — Coral reefs
6. EWB — 35

SHEET 21
1. DAB — $4.98
2. WA — Age 14 for both boys and girls
3. CB 82 — Michigan State University
4. DAH — Cornmeal and beans
5. WEN — Sunni Muslims
6. EWB — Maria Pia

SHEET 22
1. WEN — Mt. Olympus
2. DAH — To grind grain
3. WA — Genuine Risk
4. DAB — Jean Lafitte
5. CB 82 — Female roles
6. EWB — For being a spy

SHEET 23
1. DAB — He was killed by an Indian
2. CB 83 — *Crimes of the Heart*
3. DAH — President Millard Fillmore; 1850
4. WEN — Falasha or Beta Israel
5. EWB — Three times
6. WA — Tuesday

SHEET 24
1. WEN — Deforestation
2. DAH — Boston and Charleston
3. CB 82 — $800 to $3,000 per week
4. DAB — Albany
5. WA — Jack Nicklaus and Amy Alcott
6. EWB — Astrophysics

From *Cruising Through Research* © 1998 John D. Volkman. (800) 237-6124.

SHEET 25
1. WA — Rogun
2. CB 74 — Most Valuable Player
3. DAB — American Joan of Arc
4. DAH — In the *Democratic Review*
5. WEN — Honshu
6. EWB — Beethoven

SHEET 26
1. WEN — South Carolina
2. DAH — William Lloyd Garrison
3. WA — Labrador retriever
4. DAB — 1893; suicide
5. CB 83 — *Gone with the Wind*
6. EWB — Books

SHEET 27
1. CB 57 — *Picnic, Man with the Golden Arm, Eddy Duchin Story*
2. EWB — 83 years
3. DAH — Marye's
4. WA — 5,000,000 (1997)
5. DAB — 18 wives and 64 children
6. WEN — Tutsi (tallest) and Twa (Pygmies)

SHEET 28
1. EWB — India
2. DAB — Colorado
3. DAH — Two
4. WEN — Deforestation and soil erosion
5. CB 74 — Her brother, Bailey
6. WA — Mariana Trench; 35,840 ft.

SHEET 29
1. WA — *The Giver*
2. EWB — Peter
3. WEN — tropical
4. DAH — John O'Mahoney
5. CB 82 — "Snowbird"
6. DAB — Patriot spy

SHEET 30
1. EWB — Silk
2. WA — 169
3. CB 79 — *Song of Solomon*
4. DAB — Europe
5. DAH — New Orleans
6. WEN — English

From *Cruising Through Research.* © 1998 John D. Volkman. (800) 237-6124.

50 / Excursion 1: Six Basic Reference Books

SHEET 31
1. WA — 46 °F
2. DAB — The Great Renegade
3. WEN — Wolof
4. CB 69 — Asthma
5. DAH — John C. Calhoun
6. EWB — Kublai Khan

SHEET 32
1. WA — 9,117 ft.
2. DAB — Presbyterian clergyman or college president
3. WEN — Oceanic, continental, and Mediterranean
4. CB 83 — Guardian Angels
5. DAH — Three
6. EWB — Copenhagen

SHEET 33
1. WA — 1,207
2. DAB — The Gold Rush to California
3. WEN — 40
4. CB 84 — *The Ipcress File*
5. DAH — Lane Theological Seminary
6. EWB — Anthrax

SHEET 34
1. WA — 85603
2. DAB — Rose Bank
3. WEN — Roman Catholicism
4. CB 78 — New York City
5. DAH — Lawrence, Kansas
6. EWB — St. Petersburg

SHEET 35
1. ALM — Santa Barbara, CA 93108-1099
2. DAB — William H. Seward
3. WEN — Coast (costa), highlands (sierra), and jungle (selva)
4. CB 70 — Age 16
5. DAH — China
6. EWB — Seven

SHEET 36
1. WA — 12,257
2. DAB — 30 pounds
3. WEN — Dry and hot
4. CB 82 — Baseball
5. DAH — Central Intelligence Agency (CIA)
6. EWB — Age 12

From *Cruising Through Research.* © 1998 John D. Volkman. (800) 237-6124.

Excursion 2
English Reference Books

English Reference Books Instructions

Destination: English Reference Readiness

This unit is designed to challenge advanced, college-bound students. Students should have already completed the Six Basic Reference Books unit (Excursion 1, pp. 1 to 44). In this unit, students have many more books from which to choose; therefore, they need to be systematic in their searching. This lesson not only makes the students aware of a variety of reference books that they can use in English-related assignments but also stretches them mentally as they think, deduce, and search. These are real-life skills that are needed in doing college research. I use this unit with honors English freshmen, but it would also be excellent for junior and senior college-prepatory English classes.

Cargo

Overhead projector
"English Reference Books" overhead (fig. 2.1 on p. 56; can be enlarged 25% for the overhead)
"Sample Questions" overhead (fig. 2.2 on p. 57)
"English Reference Books" handout (fig. 2.1) (yellow, laminated, a class set)
"English Reference Books Annotated List" (fig. 2.3 on p. 58) (green, laminated, a class set)
36 "English Reference Questions" sheets (seven questions per sheet, one sheet per student)
Two answer keys (one for librarian and one for teacher)
Red pen (for correcting question sheets)
Three boxes (8 1/2" X 11" Xerox paper box lids work well)

52 / Excursion 2: English Reference Books

Preparation

1. Make enough copies of the "English Reference Books" handout (fig. 2.1) so that each student has a copy. I suggest that you copy them on yellow paper and laminate them so that they will last longer.

2. Make enough copies of the "English Reference Books Annotated List" handout (fig. 2.3) so that each student has a copy. I suggest that you copy them on green paper and laminate them. (Extra copies can be made of figs. 2.1 and 2.3 for students who may wish to keep them for future reference.)

3. Then provide each student with a different "English Reference Questions" sheet.

4. Make a transparency of the "Sample Questions" (fig. 2.2) and of the "English Reference Books" handout (fig 2.1). Use an overhead projector to make your presentation.

Mooring

These instructions are ideally given to the students in the vicinity of the reference section. Be sure to have the classroom teacher listen to the instructions and be available to help students as they do the lesson.

Bearings

Because the students now have basic research skills having completed Excursion 1, this presentation is much briefer and more general. The students are expected to learn about the sources as they use them. I like to point out to them that the real purpose of these questions is to familiarize them with a lot of different reference books, not just to find answers.

Navigating Through Reference Reef

1. For the first question, ask the students if the question is about the author or the book. As it is about the author, we will use the list of books under AUTHORS in figure 2.1 starting at the top of the list. Point out to the students that they can use the "English Reference Books Annotated List" (fig. 2.3) to learn more about each source. Therefore, just mention some specifics on a few of the sources. For example, demonstrate how to use the index to the *Wilson Author Series* and where the books are located. Tell the students that if they do not find the answer there, to continue through the list of sources until they do. The key is to categorize the question correctly, then go down the list of sources systematically to locate the answer.

English Reference Books Instructions / 53

2. Do not write down the sources on the overhead because you are just giving category guidelines and explaining how to use a few of the sources. Tell the students to keep track of which sources they have searched so that if they ask for help, you can determine where they are in their search. They should also fill in the name of the source in which they do find the answer.

3. For the second question, determine that the category to which it applies is BOOKS, CHARACTERS. Explain that *Masterplots* is used by looking up the title of the book.

4. For the third question, explain how to use the keyword index in the QUOTATIONS books.

5. Moving quickly through the remaining questions, determine that gobbledygook is in the category of PHRASES, SLANG; that Ah Puch is a MYTHOLOGY question; that Damocles' Sword is a LITERARY ALLUSION; and that Elijah is a BIBLICAL ALLUSION.

Crew's Special Orders

1. Before releasing the students to look up the answers, remind them to be diligent in returning the reference books to the proper shelves so that the other students can find the books. With so many books being used for this assignment, it is important for them to do this.

2. Also, show them the three boxes you have set up on a table. They are to turn in their papers in these boxes at the end of the period, finished or not. They are to put their question sheets in one box, their yellow laminated handouts in one, and their green laminated handouts in the other.

3. Then tell them to "Now go to the shelves and find the answers."

Captain's Orders

1. Most students require about two class periods to answer these questions. If students are having a problem, help them to categorize the question, and then proceed from there.

2. Correct the completed papers using the answer key. Many answers may be found in more than one source. I have indicated multiple sources whenever I am aware of them; however, there may be other sources. Therefore, when checking answers, look for the correct answer and that a likely source is indicated.

3. After two days, students will need to come in on their own time to find or correct answers; otherwise students can easily fall behind on the subsequent Queen Elizabeth assignment.

Drydock

Students who missed the presentation are given a sheet of seven questions, the yellow "English Reference Books" handout, and the green "English Reference Books Annotated List." Because they have already completed Excursion 1 and are advanced students, mention the purposes of the handouts and set them to work with the caveat to ask for assistance that if they have specific questions as they go along.

English Reference Books Bibliography

(Editor's Note: Dates are not included on this list because of the many editions and the annual editions that exist for many reference books.)

Bartlett, John. *Familiar Quotations.* Boston: Little, Brown.

Benet's Reader's Encyclopedia. New York: Harper & Row.

Brewer's Dictionary of Phrase and Fable. New York: Harper & Row.

Brownrigg, Ronald. *Who's Who in the New Testament.* New York: Holt, Rinehart & Winston.

Comay, Joan. *Who's Who in the Old Testament.* New York: Holt, Rinehart & Winston.

Cotterell, Arthur. *A Dictionary of World Mythology.* New York: G. P. Putnam's Sons.

Crabble, Margaret, ed. *Oxford Companion to English Literature.* New York: Oxford University Press.

Cuddon, J. A. *Dictionary of Literary Terms.* Garden City, New York: Doubleday.

Current Biography Yearbook. New York: H. W. Wilson.

Hart, James D., ed. *The Oxford Companion to American Literature.* New York: Oxford University Press.

Howaston, M. C., ed. *The Oxford Companion to Classical Literature.* New York: Oxford University Press.

Magill, Frank N., ed. *Cyclopedia of Literary Characters.* New York: Harper & Row.

Magill, Frank N., ed. *Cyclopedia of World Authors.* Englewood Cliffs, NJ: Salem Press.

Magill, Frank N., ed. *Magill's Quotations in Context.* Englewood Cliffs, NJ: Salem Press.

Magill, Frank N., ed. *Masterplots.* Englewood Cliffs, NJ: Salem Press.

Miller, Madeleine S., and J. Lane Miller. *Harper's Bible Dictionary.* New York: Harper & Row.

Partington, Angela, ed. *The Oxford Dictionary of Quotations.* New York: Oxford University Press.

Stevenson, Burton, ed. *The Home Book of Quotations.* New York: Dodd, Mead.

Tripp, Edward. *Crowell's Handbook of Classical Mythology.* New York: Thomas Y. Crowell.

Wilson Author Series. New York: H. W. Wilson.
    American Authors, 1600–1900.
    British Authors Before 1800.
    British Authors of the Nineteenth Century.
    European Authors, 1000–1900.
    Twentieth Century Authors.
    Twentieth Century Authors: First Supplement.
    World Authors, 1950–1970.
    World Authors, 1970–1975.
    World Authors, 1975–1980.
    World Authors, 1980–1985.
    World Authors, 1985–1990.

Zimmerman, John Edward. *Dictionary of Classical Mythology.* New York: Bantam.

English Reference Books

What kind of Question? — Which book?

BOOKS AND AUTHORS

Books, Characters
- *Masterplots, Masterplots II*
- *Oxford Companions*
- *Cyclopedia of Literary Characters*
- *Reader's Encyclopedia*

Authors
- *Wilson Author Series*
- *Cyclopedia of World Authors*
- *Current Biography*
- *Oxford Companions*

WORDS AND PHRASES

Phrases, Slang
- *Brewer's Dictionary of Phrase and Fable*
- *Reader's Encyclopedia*

Quotations
- *Bartlett's Familiar Quotations*
- *Home Book of Quotations*
- *Magill's Quotations in Context*
- *Oxford Dictionary of Quotations*

Literary Terms
- *Dictionary of Literary Terms*
- *Oxford Companions*

ALLUSIONS AND MYTHOLOGY

Literary Allusions
- *Brewer's Dictionary of Phrase and Fable*
- *Reader's Encyclopedia*
- *Oxford Companions*
- *Cyclopedia of Literary Characters*
- *Bartlett's Familiar Quotations*

Biblical Allusions
- *Harper's Bible Dictionary*
- *Who's Who in the Old Testament*
- *Who's Who in the New Testament*

Mythology
- *Crowell's Handbook of Classical Mythology*
- *Dictionary of Classical Mythology*
- *Dictionary of World Mythology*
- *Oxford Companion to Classical Literature*

From *Cruising Through Research* © 1998 John D. Volkman. (800) 237-6124.

Fig. 2.1. Make a copy for each student and laminate; make a transparency for the overhead projector.

Sample Questions

1. Ken Kesey, who wrote *One Flew Over the Cuckoo's Nest*, once served a prison term. For what charge?

   Source: _____
   Answer: _____
   _____

2. What is the name of the one-legged pirate in Robert Louis Stevenson's *Treasure Island*?

   Source: _____
   Answer: _____
   _____

3. Who wrote "Say it with flowers" before it was popularized by FTD?

   Source: _____
   Answer: _____
   _____

4. *Gobbledygook* means "unintelligible language." The term derives from the noise made by what animal?

   Source: _____
   Answer: _____
   _____

5. Ah Puch was the Mayan god of death. How was he usually portrayed?

   Source: _____
   Answer: _____
   _____

6. To what does the phrase "Damocles' Sword" refer?

   Source: _____
   Answer: _____
   _____

7. How did the Old Testament prophet Elijah die?

   Source: _____
   Answer: _____
   _____

From *Cruising Through Research.* © 1998 John D. Volkman. (800) 237-6124.

Fig. 2.2. Sample Questions. Make a transparency.

English Reference Books
Annotated List

BARTLETT'S FAMILIAR QUOTATIONS
Description: The most popular of the large collections of quotations, it includes full quotes and sources. One volume.
Hint: Arranged loosely in chronological order, it has both key-word and author indexes.

BREWER'S DICTIONARY OF PHRASE AND FABLE
Description: Defines, describes, and explains words, phrases, and allusions. Gives the origin and commonly held meaning. One volume.
Hint: Arranged in alphabetical order by important word in the phrase.

CROWELL'S HANDBOOK OF CLASSICAL MYTHOLOGY
Description: A readable explanation of the myths, characters, and places prominent in Greek and Roman literature. One volume.
Hint: Arranged alphabetically by topic.

CURRENT BIOGRAPHY
Description: Covers important contemporary (since 1940) people in all fields. Includes a photograph of the person. Published yearly since 1940. Cumulative index 1940-1995.
Hint: Use the index to find the year first; each volume is arranged alphabetically by last name.

CYCLOPEDIA OF LITERARY CHARACTERS
Description: Short descriptions of 16,000 characters that have appeared in 1,300 novels, dramas, and epics. Describes what the character did and the kind of person he or she was. One volume.
Hint: Arranged alphabetically by title of the work. Index is arranged alphabetically by the last name of the character.

CYCLOPEDIA OF WORLD AUTHORS
Description: Short biographies of world authors plus a list of their principal works. Some critical evaluation. Three volumes.
Hint: Arranged alphabetically by last name of the author.

DICTIONARY OF CLASSICAL MYTHOLOGY
Description: Comprehensive collection of information about the major myths of Greece and Rome. Includes people and places. One volume.
Hint: Arranged alphabetically by name.

From *Cruising Through Research*. © 1998 John D. Volkman. (800) 237-6124.

Fig. 2.3. Make a copy for each student and laminate.

English Reference Books Annotated List / 59

DICTIONARY OF LITERARY TERMS
Description: Contains more than 2,000 literary terms, which are defined and explained with quotations and illustrations from world literature.
Hint: Arranged alphabetically by term.

DICTIONARY OF WORLD MYTHOLOGY
Description: Provides information on major myths found in world literature. Gives factual information on gods, religious beliefs, and geographical locations. One volume.
Hint: Arranged alphabetically by section of the world, then by name.

HARPER'S BIBLE DICTIONARY
Description: Covers people, places, and events in the Bible, plus entries for archaeological and geographical topics. Includes chronologies, tables, diagrams, and color maps. One volume.
Hint: Arranged alphabetically by topic.

HOME BOOK OF QUOTATIONS
Description: A large collection of quotations, it includes full quotes and sources. One volume.
Hint: The quotes are arranged by subject; it also has keyword and author indexes.

MAGILL'S QUOTATIONS IN CONTEXT
Description: Defines and describes the origins of quotations from world literature that have become common expressions in the English language. Two sets, two volumes each.
Hint: Arranged alphabetically by major word.

MASTERPLOTS AND MASTERPLOTS II
Description: Extended summaries of the most important works in Western literature. Includes some critical evaluation. Twelve volumes and four volumes.
Hint: Arranged alphabetically by title of the work.

OXFORD COMPANION TO AMERICAN LITERATURE
Description: Treats writers and their works, literary terms, and allusions prominent in American literature. One volume.
Hint: Arranged alphabetically by topic.

OXFORD COMPANION TO CLASSICAL LITERATURE
Description: Treats writers and their works, literary terms, and allusions prominent in Greek and Roman literature. One volume.
Hint: Arranged alphabetically by topic.

OXFORD COMPANION TO ENGLISH LITERATURE
Description: Treats writers and their works, literary terms, and allusions prominent British literature. One volume.
Hint: Arranged alphabetically by topic.

Fig. 2.3 is continued on page 60.

From *Cruising Through Research.* © 1998 John D. Volkman. (800) 237-6124.

OXFORD DICTIONARY OF QUOTATIONS
Description: A comprehensive dictionary of quotations, it includes full quotes and sources. One volume.
Hint: Arranged alphabetically by author with an alphabetical key-word index.

READER'S ENCYCLOPEDIA
Description: Includes authors, their works, literary terms, and allusions. Comprehensive but entries are very short. One volume.
Hint: Arranged alphabetically by topic.

WHO'S WHO IN THE NEW TESTAMENT
Description: Describes all of the people, places, and events mentioned in the New Testament. One volume.
Hint: Arranged alphabetically by name.

WHO'S WHO IN THE OLD TESTAMENT
Description: Describes all of the people, places, and events mentioned in the Old Testament. One volume.
Hint: Arranged alphabetically by name.

WILSON AUTHOR SERIES
Description: Biographies of authors whose principal works were published in the region and/or during the time periods indicated in each volume's title.
Hint: Use the index volume first. It will indicate by abbreviations which reference volume to use. Then each volume is alphabetical by author.

English Reference Questions

Name: _____

Teacher: _____ Period: _____

Sheet 1

1. American writer William Saroyan, creator of *The Human Comedy,* wrote a hit song in 1951 with his cousin. Name the song.

   Source: _____
   Answer: _____
   _____

2. Laurence Sterne wrote one of the first true novels, *The Life and Opinions of Tristram Shandy,* in England more than 200 years ago. What happened to his body two days after he was buried?

   Source: _____
   Answer: _____
   _____

3. The term *braggadocio,* meaning "empty boasting or bragging," comes from the name of a character in what famous poem by English writer Edmond Spencer?

   Source: _____
   Answer: _____
   _____

4. One of the 12 labors of Hercules was to clean out the stables of Augeas. How quickly was Hercules to do this, and how did he do it?

   Source: _____
   Answer: _____
   _____

5. A famous quote by Oscar Wilde says that there is only one thing a poet could not survive. What was that?

   Source: _____
   Answer: _____
   _____

6. What is a *magnum opus*? From what language does this term come?

   Source: _____
   Answer: _____
   _____

7. An employer who is compared with Simon Legree is viewed as a slave driver. From what novel does this character come?

   Source: _____
   Answer: _____
   _____

From *Cruising Through Research* © 1998 John D. Volkman. (800) 237-6124.

English Reference Questions

Name: _____

Teacher: _____ Period: _____

Sheet 2

1. "Fifteen men on the Dead Man's Chest/ Yo-ho-ho, and a bottle of rum. . . ." What is the next line?

   Source: _____
   Answer: _____
   _____

2. Allen Ginsberg, a poet of the beat generation, wrote a famous poem in the 1950s that caused his publisher to be charged with obscenity. Name the poem.

   Source: _____
   Answer: _____
   _____

3. Jim Crow laws discriminate against Blacks. The term "Jim Crow" came from a Negro song. Who introduced it to Washington in 1835?

   Source: _____
   Answer: _____
   _____

4. In *Walden,* Thoreau describes life in the woods in his simple lakeside shanty. How much money did he spend "fixing it up"?

   Source: _____
   Answer: _____
   _____

5. Julia Ward Howe wrote the poem "The Battle Hymn of the Republic." How much money did she receive when it was published? Name the magazine that published it and the year.

   Source: _____
   Answer: _____
   _____

6. How many syllables and how many lines per stanza are in a "rime royal"?

   Source: _____
   Answer: _____
   _____

7. The famous "Round Table" was made by the Wizard Merlin. How many knights, if all were present, could be seated around it?

   Source: _____
   Answer: _____
   _____

From *Cruising Through Research.* © 1998 John D. Volkman. (800) 237-6124.

English Reference Questions

Name: _____

Teacher: _____ Period: _____

Sheet 3

1. Who said "Folks are better than angels" when his friends tried to comfort him as he lay dying by assuring him that he would soon be among the angels?

   Source: _____
   Answer: _____
   _____

2. When Thomas Hardy died, most of him was buried in Westminster Abbey. But where was his heart buried?

   Source: _____
   Answer: _____
   _____

3. The Old Testament talks about the plagues sent against Egypt. How many were there, and what was the last one?

   Source: _____
   Answer: _____
   _____

4. P. G. Wodehouse is an English novelist. After his first visit to the United States, he returned to London to his country home. Who kept him company there?

   Source: _____
   Answer: _____
   _____

5. In Mark Twain's *A Connecticut Yankee in King Arthur's Court* a spell is cast on the Boss. How many years was he to sleep?

   Source: _____
   Answer: _____
   _____

6. A sonnet is a patterned poem. How many lines are in a sonnet, and what is the meter?

   Source: _____
   Answer: _____
   _____

7. When Theseus navigated the labyrinth to kill the Minotaur, he was aided by Ariadne. What did she give him that enabled him to return safely?

   Source: _____
   Answer: _____
   _____

From *Cruising Through Research.* © 1998 John D. Volkman. (800) 237-6124.

64 / Excursion 2: English Reference Books

English Reference Questions

Name: _____

Teacher: _____ Period: _____

Sheet 4

1. What author wrote the saying "Clear as a bell"?

   Source: _____
   Answer: _____
   _____

2. Many people have heard of Edward Lear, an English author of the 1800s, who wrote nonsense verses and limericks. How many children were in his family?

   Source: _____
   Answer: _____
   _____

3. How old was English poet and critic Elizabeth Jennings when she wrote her first poem?

   Source: _____
   Answer: _____
   _____

4. *The Catcher in the Rye* is a favorite book of high school students. Name the rebellious teenager and his sister.

   Source: _____
   Answer: _____
   _____

5. In Shakespeare's play *Julius Caesar* a soothsayer tells Caesar to "Beware the Ides of March." What were the ides that Shakespeare was referring to?

   Source: _____
   Answer: _____
   _____

6. *The Man Without a Country* was originally written as a propaganda for a bitterly fought Ohio governor's campaign? Give the year.

   Source: _____
   Answer: _____
   _____

7. Horus was an Egyptian sun or sky god, similar to the Greek Apollo. Apollo is represented as a handsome young man. What does Horus's head look like?

   Source: _____
   Answer: _____
   _____

From *Cruising Through Research* © 1998 John D. Volkman. (800) 237-6124.

English Reference Questions

Name: _____

Teacher: _____ Period: _____

Sheet 5

1. At the inauguration of President Kennedy in 1961, Robert Frost read a poem containing the line "The land was ours before we were the land's." What was the poem?

   Source: _____
   Answer: _____
   _____

2. How many brothers and sisters did American writer Stephen Crane have?

   Source: _____
   Answer: _____
   _____

3. In *Alcestis*, a play by Euripides (438 B.C.), King Admetus can escape death if he finds someone to die for him. Who offers to take his place?

   Source: _____
   Answer: _____
   _____

4. Dorothy Sayers, creator of the English detective Lord Peter Wimsey, was one of the first women to receive a degree from Oxford. When did she receive it, and in what field?

   Source: _____
   Answer: _____
   _____

5. *Looking Backward*, the novel by Edward Bellamy, presents a Socialist Utopia. In what year does the leading character awake, and who discovers him?

   Source: _____
   Answer: _____
   _____

6. When Judas Iscariot betrayed Jesus with a kiss, how many pieces of silver was he given, and what did he do with them?

   Source: _____
   Answer: _____
   _____

7. Thor, Norse god of thunder, always wore a pair of iron gloves to grasp what magical tool?

   Source: _____
   Answer: _____
   _____

From *Cruising Through Research* © 1998 John D. Volkman. (800) 237-6124.

English Reference Questions

Name: _____

Teacher: _____ Period: _____

Sheet 6

1. In the phrase "Sukey, take it off again," to what does "it" refer?

    Source: _____
    Answer: _____
    _____

2. Gordon Parks, former *Life* photographer and author of *The Learning Tree*, was the youngest of how many children?

    Source: _____
    Answer: _____
    _____

3. William Saroyan, who was born in Fresno, California, received the Pulitzer Prize for Drama in 1940. As a youngster, how many books did he read in the public library?

    Source: _____
    Answer: _____
    _____

4. James Hilton, a popular British author, was born in 1900. How old was he when his first novel was published?

    Source: _____
    Answer: _____
    _____

5. Asa was the third King of Judah in the Bible. How long did his reign last?

    Source: _____
    Answer: _____
    _____

6. Raskolnikov, the major character in the Russian novel *Crime and Punishment*, kills an old woman seemingly for no reason. For how long is he sentenced to Siberia?

    Source: _____
    Answer: _____
    _____

7. Apollo was the Greek god of music, prophesy, and healing. What was the name of his father?

    Source: _____
    Answer: _____
    _____

From *Cruising Through Research* © 1998 John D. Volkman. (800) 237-6124.

English Reference Questions

Name: _____

Teacher: _____ Period: _____

Sheet 7

1. Who said, "I expect that woman will be the last thing civilized by man"?

   Source: _____
   Answer: _____
   _____

2. In what year did Ursula Le Guin win the National Book Award for *The Farthest Shore*? For what kind of fiction books is she best known?

   Source: _____
   Answer: _____
   _____

3. How old was Langston Hughes when he wrote *The Wary Blues* in 1926?

   Source: _____
   Answer: _____
   _____

4. A haiku is a Japanese poem of three lines with 17 syllables. How many lines and syllables are in a tanka?

   Source: _____
   Answer: _____
   _____

5. In New Testament times, the Roman Empire maintained numerous legions of soldiers in what is today the Middle East. How many soldiers were in a legion?

   Source: _____
   Answer: _____
   _____

6. In Graham Greene's *The Heart of the Matter*, what kind of a reputation does Major Scobie have?

   Source: _____
   Answer: _____
   _____

7. Arachne, a superb weaver, challenged the goddess Athena to a weaving contest. Arachne's cloth was so perfect that Athena, in a fury, changed her into what?

   Source: _____
   Answer: _____
   _____

From *Cruising Through Research* © 1998 John D. Volkman. (800) 237-6124.

68 / Excursion 2: English Reference Books

English Reference Questions

Name: _____

Teacher: _____ Period: _____

Sheet 8

1. The line "Fifteen men on the deadman's chest" is sung by a drunken sea captain. What was his one concern?

   Source: _____
   Answer: _____
   _____

2. One of the most famous American authors in the 1800s was Richard Henry Dana Jr. His best-known book was a travel diary. Name it.

   Source: _____
   Answer: _____
   _____

3. The German writer of *All Quiet on the Western Front*, Erich Remarque, actually fought in World War I. How many times was he wounded?

   Source: _____
   Answer: _____
   _____

4. Calling a favored child a "Benjamin" is a Biblical allusion to Jacob's youngest son. How much larger was Benjamin's share at the Egyptian banquet?

   Source: _____
   Answer: _____
   _____

5. The Latin *quar* means "four." How many pages are in a book called a quarto?

   Source: _____
   Answer: _____
   _____

6. Jean Valjean, the central figure in Victor Hugo's *Les Miserables*, was originally sent to prison for stealing what for his sister's family?

   Source: _____
   Answer: _____
   _____

7. The term "the Gordian knot" refers to any complicated problem or deadlock. Who was the famous Greek ruler who solved the problem by cutting the knot?

   Source: _____
   Answer: _____
   _____

From *Cruising Through Research* © 1998 John D. Volkman. (800) 237-6124.

English Reference Questions

Name: _____

Teacher: _____ Period: _____

Sheet 9

1. Who wrote, "It is not worthwhile to go round the world to count the cats in Zanzibar"?

   Source: _____
   Answer: _____
   _____

2. John Greenleaf Whittier, an American poet, worked on the family farm until he received one year of higher education at Haverhill Academy. How old was he then?

   Source: _____
   Answer: _____
   _____

3. Judith Martin writes a newspaper column called "Miss Manners." Why does she say she writes about etiquette?

   Source: _____
   Answer: _____
   _____

4. The phrase "Lining of the pocket" refers to money. Who originally obtained a dress-coat lined with banknotes?

   Source: _____
   Answer: _____
   _____

5. In what literary work was the phrase "as good as gold" first used, and what character said it?

   Source: _____
   Answer: _____
   _____

6. In Mark Twain's *The Prince and the Pauper*, Tom Canty is the name of the pauper. What is the name of the prince?

   Source: _____
   Answer: _____
   _____

7. Tezcatlipoca demanded blood sacrifices. Annually, the handsomest man was heaped with pleasure, then his living heart cut out. In what mythology is this god?

   Source: _____
   Answer: _____
   _____

From *Cruising Through Research* © 1998 John D. Volkman. (800) 237-6124.

English Reference Questions

Name: _____

Teacher: _____ Period: _____

Sheet 10

1. What novel begins with the line, "Call me Ishmael"?

   Source: _____
   Answer: _____
   _____

2. Cotton Mather was a Puritan and a child prodigy. He entered Harvard at age 12 and wrote more than 400 books. How many wives and children did he have?

   Source: _____
   Answer: _____
   _____

3. In the Old Testament, how long was Jacob supposed to work before he could marry his love, Rachel? How long did he actually work?

   Source: _____
   Answer: _____
   _____

4. Author James Michener was said to be an academic bum and a confirmed traveler. How many universities did he attend?

   Source: _____
   Answer: _____
   _____

5. Muckraking (public exposure of misconduct) originally alluded to a character in a novel who was so intent on raking up muck he could not see a crown. What is the novel and the author's name?

   Source: _____
   Answer: _____
   _____

6. Who wrote, "Tis better to have loved and lost than never to have loved at all"?

   Source: _____
   Answer: _____
   _____

7. Dolius was a servant in Greek legend famous not for what he did but for the master to whom he remained faithful for many years. Name the master.

   Source: _____
   Answer: _____
   _____

From *Cruising Through Research*. © 1998 John D. Volkman. (800) 237-6124.

English Reference Questions

Name: _____

Teacher: _____ Period: _____

Sheet 11

1. In the early 1800s, John Lewis Burckhart wrote famous travel books in English about his explorations in Africa. How old was he when he died?

   Source: _____
   Answer: _____
   _____

2. How many *people* were saved on Noah's Ark during the flood, and who were they?

   Source: _____
   Answer: _____
   _____

3. Carson McCullers was an American author, but her original ambition was to be what?

   Source: _____
   Answer: _____
   _____

4. "You're a better man than I am, Gunga Din!" is a famous line from one of Rudyard Kipling's poems. Who was Gunga Din, and what happened to him in the poem?

   Source: _____
   Answer: _____
   _____

5. In Mark Twain's *A Connecticut Yankee in King Arthur's Court*, the hero is saved from death at the stake because of what prediction he made?

   Source: _____
   Answer: _____
   _____

6. Midas was a king in Greek myth whose touch turned everything to gold. How was he "cured" of this "blessing"? What kind of ears did he have?

   Source: _____
   Answer: _____
   _____

7. Who wrote, "And all the flowers were mine"?

   Source: _____
   Answer: _____
   _____

From *Cruising Through Research* © 1998 John D. Volkman. (800) 237-6124.

English Reference Questions

Name: _____

Teacher: _____ Period: _____

Sheet 12

1. Stoning was the ordinary method of capital punishment under Hebrew law in biblical times. Name three offenses punishable by stoning.

   Source: _____
   Answer: _____
   _____

2. Beginning in 1918, Western author William MacLeod Raine averaged two books a year for almost 40 years. Name the first book he published and the year.

   Source: _____
   Answer: _____
   _____

3. English poet Percy Shelley married Harriet Westbrook when she was 16 and left her 3 years later. Two years later, Harriet drowned herself. How did Shelley die?

   Source: _____
   Answer: _____
   _____

4. A cynical poet said, "Malt does more than Milton can, to justify God's ways to man." Who is the poet, and what is his poem?

   Source: _____
   Answer: _____
   _____

5. When Adolph Ochs bought the *New York Times* in 1896, he adopted a motto which has been printed in each edition since. What is the motto?

   Source: _____
   Answer: _____
   _____

6. Who is Count Alezey Kirilich Vronnsky, and in what novel does he appear?

   Source: _____
   Answer: _____
   _____

7. In Hindu mythology, Amrita was the water of life. What is the literal meaning of *amrita*?

   Source: _____
   Answer: _____
   _____

From *Cruising Through Research* © 1998 John D. Volkman. (800) 237-6124.

English Reference Questions

Name: _____

Teacher: _____ Period: _____

Sheet 13

1. Not many children today read books by American author Harriet Lothrop, but she was very popular in the late 1800s. What was the title of her most famous book?

   Source: _____
   Answer: _____
   _____

2. What does the phrase "a storm in a teapot" mean?

   Source: _____
   Answer: _____
   _____

3. Carl Sandburg spent approximately 15 years sitting at a typewriter perched on a cracker box in his attic writing the biography of what American?

   Source: _____
   Answer: _____
   _____

4. Crossed rhyme occurs in long couplets. What does it mean?

   Source: _____
   Answer: _____
   _____

5. In Thomas Ady's famous poem "A Candle in the Dark," he talks about angels: "One to watch, and one to pray." What is the next line of the poem?

   Source: _____
   Answer: _____
   _____

6. In *The Three Musketeers* by Alexandre Dumas, there are actually four adventurers. What were the names of the three musketeers and their comrade?

   Source: _____
   Answer: _____
   _____

7. When an angry Zeus tried to destroy the human race with a great flood, what did Deucalion, son of Prometheus, do?

   Source: _____
   Answer: _____
   _____

From *Cruising Through Research.* © 1998 John D. Volkman. (800) 237-6124.

English Reference Questions

Name: _____

Teacher: _____ Period: _____

Sheet 14

1. Michael Crichton wrote *Jurassic Park*. What medical school was he attending when he originally started writing?

   Source: _____
   Answer: _____
   _____

2. Dog days are days when the temperature is very high. In the phrase, the dog does not refer to an animal but to something else. Name it.

   Source: _____
   Answer: _____
   _____

3. Dee Brown, author of *Creek Mary's Blood*, began his writing career as a journalist. What kind of stories did he cover?

   Source: _____
   Answer: _____
   _____

4. In the Bible, Herodias helped secure the execution of what prophet?

   Source: _____
   Answer: _____
   _____

5. In describing the power of love, what book says, "Love is strong as death; jealousy is cruel as the grave"?

   Source: _____
   Answer: _____
   _____

6. In the modern classic *Green Mansions*, the main character is a strange, birdlike girl. What is her name?

   Source: _____
   Answer: _____
   _____

7. In Roman religion, vestal virgins were caretakers of the sacred fire. What happened to the vestal virgins if they lost their virginity?

   Source: _____
   Answer: _____
   _____

From *Cruising Through Research* © 1998 John D. Volkman. (800) 237-6124.

English Reference Questions

Name: _____

Teacher: _____ Period: _____

Sheet 15

1. Garrison Keillor is the author of the 1985 best-seller *Lake Wobegon Days*. His real name is Gary. When did he change it and why?

   Source: _____
   Answer: _____
   _____

2. "To let the cat out of the bag" means to reveal a secret, but originally it referred to a trick in which a cat was switched for another animal. Name the animal.

   Source: _____
   Answer: _____
   _____

3. William Dean Howells wrote *The Rise of Silas Lapham* in 1885. As a boy, he rarely lived in one town for very long. Why did his family move so often?

   Source: _____
   Answer: _____
   _____

4. In the Bible, what does the name David mean?

   Source: _____
   Answer: _____
   _____

5. In a famous poem, a sailor adrift on a ship "Cried, a sail, a sail!" What had this sailor done in the line above? Name the poem.

   Source: _____
   Answer: _____
   _____

6. In Edmund Spenser's *The Faerie Queen,* Gloriana is an idealized portrait of whom?

   Source: _____
   Answer: _____
   _____

7. Daphne, the beautiful and chaste river nymph, refused to be seduced by the charms of Apollo. In Greek mythology, how did she escape?

   Source: _____
   Answer: _____
   _____

From *Cruising Through Research* © 1998 John D. Volkman. (800) 237-6124.

76 / Excursion 2: English Reference Books

English Reference Questions

Name: _____

Teacher: _____ Period: _____

Sheet 16

1. Henry Longfellow wrote about his pain in the poem "Cross of Snow" 18 years after his second wife died. What was the cause of her death?

    Source: _____
    Answer: _____
    _____

2. In Greek mythology, Chiron was the son of Cronus and Philyra. What else was he?

    Source: _____
    Answer: _____
    _____

3. When French novelist Honore de Balzac was 51, he married a younger girl. How old was she?

    Source: _____
    Answer: _____
    _____

4. You have probably heard the expression "old as Methuselah." Where does the phrase come from, and how old was Methuselah when he died?

    Source: _____
    Answer: _____
    _____

5. Whom was poet Alfred Lord Tennyson referring to in the lines "Theirs not to reason why, Theirs but to do or die"?

    Source: _____
    Answer: _____
    _____

6. In John Steinbeck's novel *In Dubious Battle*, of what group did Jim Nolan become a member?

    Source: _____
    Answer: _____
    _____

7. Codrus was a legendary king of Athens. How did he save the city from an attack by the Dorians?

    Source: _____
    Answer: _____
    _____

From *Cruising Through Research* © 1998 John D. Volkman. (800) 237-6124.

English Reference Questions

Name: _____

Teacher: _____ Period: _____

Sheet 17

1. Novelist Iris Murdoch can also be described as a professional in what other field?

   Source: _____
   Answer: _____
   _____

2. An anagram is a new word formed from the same letters as another word. What is a palindrome? Give an example of one.

   Source: _____
   Answer: _____
   _____

3. Although Arthur Koestler is known as a novelist, in 1931 he was the only newspaperman aboard the *Graf Zeppelin* on its Arctic expedition. Name the newspaper for which he worked.

   Source: _____
   Answer: _____
   _____

4. Shakespeare's play *The Tempest* has a misshapen creature similar to Quasimodo in *The Hunchback of Notre Dame*. Who is the brute in *The Tempest*? What are his tasks?

   Source: _____
   Answer: _____
   _____

5. The astrological sign of Gemini is represented by the twins. Gemini originally came from Greek myth. What were the names of those twins?

   Source: _____
   Answer: _____
   _____

6. The Iran-Contra scandal calls to mind the famous line "Patriotism is the last refuge of a scoundrel." Who said it?

   Source: _____
   Answer: _____
   _____

7. The Four Horsemen of the Apocalypse are literary personifications of the evils of war. Name the four Horsemen.

   Source: _____
   Answer: _____
   _____

From *Cruising Through Research* © 1998 John D. Volkman. (800) 237-6124.

English Reference Questions

Name: _____

Teacher: _____ Period: _____

Sheet 18

1. Mary Wollstonecraft Godwin, an English feminist, wrote *A Vindication of the Rights of Woman* in 1792. It's no wonder, considering what her father was. What was he?

   Source: _____
   Answer: _____
   _____

2. "Sour grapes" is a phrase often used to describe a negative attitude. From where did this expression originate?

   Source: _____
   Answer: _____
   _____

3. Why did poet Louis Untermeyer leave high school at the age of 15?

   Source: _____
   Answer: _____
   _____

4. Prometheus is known as the one who stole fire from Olympus and gave it to mankind. What was his punishment for doing so?

   Source: _____
   Answer: _____
   _____

5. The command "Don't give up the ship!" is often attributed to John Paul Jones. Who actually said it?

   Source: _____
   Answer: _____
   _____

6. In *The Three Musketeers* by Alexandre Dumas there are actually four adventurers. Name the women with whom the fourth adventurer falls in love.

   Source: _____
   Answer: _____
   _____

7. Solomon is known in the Old Testament for his riches and his wisdom. Who were his parents?

   Source: _____
   Answer: _____
   _____

From *Cruising Through Research* © 1998 John D. Volkman. (800) 237-6124.

English Reference Questions

Name: _____

Teacher: _____ Period: _____

Sheet 19

1. Norman Mailer, author of the 1940s novel *The Naked and the Dead*, graduated *cum laude* from Harvard in what field?

   Source: _____
   Answer: _____
   _____

2. In the *Trojan Women* by Euripides, who is Astyanax? What is his fate?

   Source: _____
   Answer: _____
   _____

3. Ved Mehta first became famous for his autobiography in the 1960s. He has a disability which he never mentions in his books. What is it?

   Source: _____
   Answer: _____
   _____

4. The goddess Sedna holds an important place in the mythology and traditions of the Eskimos. What happened to her fingers?

   Source: _____
   Answer: _____
   _____

5. Uriah Heep is one of the most famous characters in fiction. Name the book in which he appears.

   Source: _____
   Answer: _____
   _____

6. The term *Catch-22* comes from a book by the same name written by Joseph Heller. What is the name of the captain, who is the main character?

   Source: _____
   Answer: _____
   _____

7. Who said, "Good wits, you know, have short memories"?

   Source: _____
   Answer: _____
   _____

From *Cruising Through Research* © 1998 John D. Volkman. (800) 237-6124.

English Reference Questions

Name: _____

Teacher: _____ Period: _____

Sheet 20

1. Daniel Defoe's *Robinson Crusoe* is based on the adventures of a real person who, at his own request, was put ashore on an uninhabited island. What was the man's name?

   Source: _____
   Answer: _____
   _____

2. In medieval universities, four subjects, known collectively as the quadrivium, were studied by those pursuing the Master of Arts degree. Name the four subjects.

   Source: _____
   Answer: _____
   _____

3. Aldous Huxley, author of *Brave New World*, switched from the study of medicine to literature due to a physical disability he developed at the age of 18. What was it?

   Source: _____
   Answer: _____
   _____

4. Lysistrata, in Aristophanes's play of the same name, proposes what to the women of Greece to end the war?

   Source: _____
   Answer: _____
   _____

5. *After the First Death* is the title of a novel by Robert Cormier. The title comes from a line of an earlier author. Who was the author and what is the rest of the line?

   Source: _____
   Answer: _____
   _____

6. Elijah prophesied a gruesome end for Jezebel, a wicked woman in the Old Testament. How was she killed?

   Source: _____
   Answer: _____
   _____

7. In the famous Russian novel *Anna Karenina*, the character after whom the novel is named commits suicide at the end of the story. How did she die?

   Source: _____
   Answer: _____
   _____

From *Cruising Through Research* © 1998 John D. Volkman. (800) 237-6124.

English Reference Questions

Name: _____

Teacher: _____ Period: _____

Sheet 21

1. Teenagers like *I Never Promised You a Rose Garden*, a novel about author Joanne Greenberg's ordeal in a mental hospital. Why was she persecuted in her childhood?

   Source: _____
   Answer: _____
   _____

2. William Holmes McGuffey is best known for his reading textbooks which were published in the 1830s. He was also a minister. What was so unusual about his more than 3,000 sermons?

   Source: _____
   Answer: _____
   _____

3. Goops were created by American Gelett Burgess (1866–1951) for a magazine, and he later used them in children's books to teach manners. What are they?

   Source: _____
   Answer: _____
   _____

4. A repetitive and difficult task is known as a Sisyphean labor. In Greek legend, what task did Sisyphus have to perform?

   Source: _____
   Answer: _____
   _____

5. What American humorist wrote, "*Classic*: A book which people praise and don't read"?

   Source: _____
   Answer: _____
   _____

6. The biblical Job is known for his patience. Name the three friends whom the Old Testament states came to visit him when he was suffering through terrible times.

   Source: _____
   Answer: _____
   _____

7. Quasimodo is the major character in *The Hunchback of Notre Dame*. With whom does he fall in love, and what happens to her in the end?

   Source: _____
   Answer: _____
   _____

From *Cruising Through Research* © 1998 John D. Volkman. (800) 237-6124.

English Reference Questions

Name: _____

Teacher: _____ Period: _____

Sheet 22

1. James Russell Lowell, American poet and critic, was also U.S. Minister to Spain in 1877. He was the first editor of what well-known American periodical?

    Source: _____
    Answer: _____
    _____

2. In ancient and medieval physiology and in literature, we find references to four liquids of the body called humours. What were the four humours?

    Source: _____
    Answer: _____
    _____

3. Stephan Zweig, an Austrian writer, committed suicide because of loneliness and despair over World War II. Where was he when he committed suicide?

    Source: _____
    Answer: _____
    _____

4. Who rode Pegasus, the winged horse in Greek mythology, during his famous exploits?

    Source: _____
    Answer: _____
    _____

5. Some people think that the phrase "The pen is mightier than the sword" came from the American Revolution. Who was the actual author?

    Source: _____
    Answer: _____
    _____

6. In the Old Testament, Jacob is known for the ladder he saw during a night vision. Who was Jacob's twin brother?

    Source: _____
    Answer: _____
    _____

7. In *The Barber of Seville*, what is the barber's name?

    Source: _____
    Answer: _____
    _____

From *Cruising Through Research* © 1998 John D. Volkman. (800) 237-6124.

English Reference Questions

Name: _____

Teacher: _____ Period: _____

Sheet 23

1. Emma Southworth was an American novelist in the 1800s. John Greenleaf Whittier wrote a ballad based on an idea suggested by Mrs. Southworth. Name the ballad.

   Source: _____
   Answer: _____
   _____

2. Herman McNeile, a British writer who fought in World War I, was the creator of a very famous detective whose name is almost as good as Mike Hammer. Name the detective.

   Source: _____
   Answer: _____
   _____

3. Give two examples of words that are onomatopoeic.

   Source: _____
   Answer: _____
   _____

4. Icarus is known for making his escape from Crete using wax wings. Sadly, he flew too close to the sun and fell to his death. Name Icarus's famous father.

   Source: _____
   Answer: _____
   _____

5. "This happy breed of men, this little world, this precious stone set in the silver sea" is what country described by what author in what work?

   Source: _____
   Answer: _____
   _____

6. In E. M. Forster's novel *A Room with a View*, Lucy witnesses a stabbing. Who else witnessed it?

   Source: _____
   Answer: _____
   _____

7. According to the Bible, the Garden of Eden was well watered by four rivers. Two of those rivers have been positively identified as rivers we know today. Name them.

   Source: _____
   Answer: _____
   _____

From *Cruising Through Research*. © 1998 John D. Volkman. (800) 237-6124.

English Reference Questions

Name: _____

Teacher: _____ Period: _____

Sheet 24

1. The phrase *carpe diem* is used to describe the literary theme of "seizing the moment." Where in ancient literature is it found?

   Source: _____
   Answer: _____
   _____

2. Thomas Wolfe, author of *Look Homeward, Angel*, returned from England in the 1920s and wrote each night, living on a terrible diet. Of what did it consist?

   Source: _____
   Answer: _____
   _____

3. In Greek legend, who built the labyrinth in which the Minotaur was kept?

   Source: _____
   Answer: _____
   _____

4. What author wrote, "The virtue lies in the struggle, not the prize"?

   Source: _____
   Answer: _____
   _____

5. In the story *Swiss Family Robinson*, what were the names of the four sons who were shipwrecked?

   Source: _____
   Answer: _____
   _____

6. In the Old Testament, obedience was a very important trait. What happened to Queen Vashti when she didn't obey the King's demands?

   Source: _____
   Answer: _____
   _____

7. American poet Philip Levine was also a professor at Fresno State University. Where was he born?

   Source: _____
   Answer: _____
   _____

From *Cruising Through Research.* © 1998 John D. Volkman. (800) 237-6124.

English Reference Questions

Name: _____

Teacher: _____ Period: _____

Sheet 25

1. *The French Lieutenant's Woman* was written by John Fowles and later made into a movie. But, interestingly, Fowles is not French. What nationality is he?

   Source: _____
   Answer: _____
   _____

2. In Greek mythology, Myrrha was changed into a tree as a result of an incestuous affair with her father. Name the tree.

   Source: _____
   Answer: _____
   _____

3. British author C. S. Lewis is best known to Americans for *The Chronicles of Narnia*. He wrote his first book under another name. What was it?

   Source: _____
   Answer: _____
   _____

4. In Persian mythology, Mithra was both a creator and a terrible war god who had four special weapons. Name them.

   Source: _____
   Answer: _____
   _____

5. Who said, "Some books are to be tasted, others to be swallowed, and some few to be chewed and digested"?

   Source: _____
   Answer: _____
   _____

6. "Evangeline" was written by Henry Wadsworth Longfellow. Who is Evangeline's lover, and where does she finally find him?

   Source: _____
   Answer: _____
   _____

7. To refer to acquaintances encountered only once, the expression "ships that pass in the night" is often used. From what author and work does this phrase come?

   Source: _____
   Answer: _____
   _____

From *Cruising Through Research* © 1998 John D. Volkman. (800) 237-6124.

English Reference Questions

Name: _____

Teacher: _____ Period: _____

Sheet 26

1. Although Arthur Koestler wrote in English, he was not born in the United States. Where was he born?

    Source: _____
    Answer: _____
    _____

2. Sherwood Anderson, an American writer in the 1930s, died as a result of swallowing a toothpick while at a cocktail party. In what city did he die?

    Source: _____
    Answer: _____
    _____

3. *Bylina* is a Russian term for an epic or heroic folk song. What kind of verse is it in?

    Source: _____
    Answer: _____
    _____

4. Ceres is the Roman name for what Greek goddess?

    Source: _____
    Answer: _____
    _____

5. In Joseph Heller's novel *Catch-22*, Yossarian is asked, "Where are the snows of yesteryear?" Name the poem and the author of that original question.

    Source: _____
    Answer: _____
    _____

6. What was the one fault Sir Gawain manifested in the testing sequence at the end of *Sir Gawain and the Green Knight*?

    Source: _____
    Answer: _____
    _____

7. During the era of the Old Testament, what was a scourge, and when was it used?

    Source: _____
    Answer: _____
    _____

From *Cruising Through Research* © 1998 John D. Volkman. (800) 237-6124.

English Reference Questions

Name: _____

Teacher: _____ Period: _____

Sheet 27

1. Cervantes, the well-known Spanish author of *Don Quixote*, started out as a soldier. He fought in the naval battle of Lepanto in 1571. In what part of his body was he wounded?

   Source: _____
   Answer: _____
   _____

2. Oliver La Farge, author of *Laughing Boy* and other works about the American Indians, was named after a relative, a famous naval officer. Who was he?

   Source: _____
   Answer: _____
   _____

3. A song in Sir W. S. Gilbert's *H.M.S. Pinafore* begins, "Things are not what they seem." What other author used the same line?

   Source: _____
   Answer: _____
   _____

4. The labyrinth in classical mythology is probably derived from the word *labrys*, which means what?

   Source: _____
   Answer: _____
   _____

5. The original *Frankenstein* was written by Mary Shelley in 1818. Name the town in the book in which Frankenstein supposedly lived.

   Source: _____
   Answer: _____
   _____

6. Father Latour, a priest in *Death Comes to an Archbishop*, often employed an intelligent young Indian named Jacinto. What was Jacinto's job?

   Source: _____
   Answer: _____
   _____

7. When the "owl and the pussycat went to sea in a beautiful pea green boat," what did they take with them?

   Source: _____
   Answer: _____
   _____

From *Cruising Through Research* © 1998 John D. Volkman. (800) 237-6124.

88 / Excursion 2: English Reference Books

English Reference Questions

Name: _____

Teacher: _____ Period: _____

Sheet 28

1. Julia Ward Howe wrote the poem "The Battle Hymn of the Republic." By what nicknames did she and her husband call each other?

   Source: _____
   Answer: _____
   _____

2. American mystery writer Tony Hillerman includes much about Native American culture in his novels. That is because he grew up with Seminoles and Blackfeet in what town in Oklahoma?

   Source: _____
   Answer: _____
   _____

3. The daily press is known as the Fourth Estate. What are the other three?

   Source: _____
   Answer: _____
   _____

4. The word *nemesis* means "unbeatable rival." In Greek myth, who was Nemesis?

   Source: _____
   Answer: _____
   _____

5. When Plato wrote *The Republic,* he outlined the three classes of citizens and compared them to the three elements in a just man. Name all six.

   Source: _____
   Answer: _____
   _____

6. The closest companions to Frankie Addams, a character in *The Member of the Wedding* by Carson McCullers, are her little cousin and her surrogate mother. Name them.

   Source: _____
   Answer: _____
   _____

7. The following quote has become part of several songs: "O death, where is thy sting? O grave, where is thy victory?" Where did this quotation originate?

   Source: _____
   Answer: _____
   _____

From *Cruising Through Research* © 1998 John D. Volkman. (800) 237-6124.

English Reference Questions

Name: _____

Teacher: _____ Period: _____

Sheet 29

1. Ezra Pound lived in Europe for 40 years as a "voluntary exile" from the United States. What event caused his sudden return to the United States in 1945?

   Source: _____
   Answer: _____
   _____

2. George Moore, an Irish author in the early 1900s, would not have gone to school if his father had not won a lot of money in a horse race. Name the horse.

   Source: _____
   Answer: _____
   _____

3. One of the characters in *Brideshead Revisited* is named Kurt. How does he die?

   Source: _____
   Answer: _____
   _____

4. The Greeks believed that the song of the Sirens was irresistible. Name the ship that Butes jumped off so that he could swim to them.

   Source: _____
   Answer: _____
   _____

5. *Absalom, Absalom* is a novel about the American South. The title comes from a person in the Old Testament who kills someone. Whom does Absalom kill?

   Source: _____
   Answer: _____
   _____

6. The last line of the inscription found at the base of the Statue of Liberty reads, "I lift my lamp beside the golden door." Who wrote the inscription?

   Source: _____
   Answer: _____
   _____

7. The term *halcyon days* (times of peace and prosperity) comes from the name of what bird that was thought to nest on the surface of the sea when it was calm?

   Source: _____
   Answer: _____
   _____

From *Cruising Through Research* © 1998 John D. Volkman. (800) 237-6124.

90 / Excursion 2: English Reference Books

English Reference Questions

Name: _____

Teacher: _____ Period: _____

Sheet 30

1. As a young man, Benjamin Disraeli, later Prime Minister of England, debated between a political and literary career. What was the name of his sensational first novel?

    Source: _____
    Answer: _____
    _____

2. O. Henry, who died in 1910, wrote one of his most famous works while in prison. For what was he convicted?

    Source: _____
    Answer: _____
    _____

3. Cincinnatus Miller ran away to the California gold mines when he was 15. How did this writer get his first name?

    Source: _____
    Answer: _____
    _____

4. After Lemuel Gulliver, the character in Jonathan Swift's book *Gulliver's Travels*, returns from his last voyage, his wife kisses him and he does what?

    Source: _____
    Answer: _____
    _____

5. Tennyson's poem "The Lotos-Eaters" is a reference to classical mythology. Who visits the lotos eaters, and how does the fruit affect its eaters?

    Source: _____
    Answer: _____
    _____

6. *The Beggar's Opera* is a musical play by what English playwright?

    Source: _____
    Answer: _____
    _____

7. "Joy to the World! the Lord is come" is the first line of a popular Christmas song written in 1719. Who wrote it, and upon what biblical psalm was it based?

    Source: _____
    Answer: _____
    _____

From *Cruising Through Research* © 1998 John D. Volkman. (800) 237-6124.

English Reference Questions

Name: _____

Teacher: _____ Period: _____

Sheet 31

1. Thomas Paine, firebrand author of *Common Sense,* was apprenticed to what trade at the age of 12?

   Source: _____
   Answer: _____
   _____

2. Leon Uris has written many books based on his own experiences. Which novel of his was published in 1953 and then sold to Hollywood?

   Source: _____
   Answer: _____
   _____

3. How many lines does a limerick have? What is its rhyming scheme, and from what country did it originate?

   Source: _____
   Answer: _____
   _____

4. In Remarque's *All Quiet on the Western Front,* what did Muller get when Kemerich died?

   Source: _____
   Answer: _____
   _____

5. According to Greek mythology, what caused Orpheus to lose his wife a second time to the underworld?

   Source: _____
   Answer: _____
   _____

6. The phrase "the lion's share" means the bulk of or nearly all. The spoils of the hunt are broken into fourths. Name the four portions.

   Source: _____
   Answer: _____
   _____

7. From what play does the quote "When ingratitude barbs the dart of injury, the wound has double danger in it" come?

   Source: _____
   Answer: _____
   _____

From *Cruising Through Research* © 1998 John D. Volkman. (800) 237-6124.

English Reference Questions

Name: _____

Teacher: _____ Period: _____

Sheet 32

1. John le Carré is a pseudonym; what is the author's real name?

   Source: _____
   Answer: _____
   _____

2. A haiku is a form of Japanese poetry that has three lines. How many syllables are supposed to be on each line?

   Source: _____
   Answer: _____
   _____

3. The hero of *The Fountainhead*, a 1943 novel by Ayn Rand, is supposed to be modeled on a famous American architect. Who?

   Source: _____
   Answer: _____
   _____

4. In *The Pit* by Frank Norris, Curtis Jadwin, a speculator in wheat, was spoken of as the "unknown bull." Why was he called that?

   Source: _____
   Answer: _____
   _____

5. In Greek and Roman mythology, Echo was a nymph. Who was the goddess who took away from Echo the power of normal speech?

   Source: _____
   Answer: _____
   _____

6. Natty Bumppo is a central character in five novels; in each he has a different name: Deerslayer, Hawkeye, the Trapper, Pathfinder, and Leatherstocking. Who wrote the novels?

   Source: _____
   Answer: _____
   _____

7. Thomas Carlyle said, "History is the essence of innumerable biographies." Who expressed the same idea with the statement "There is properly no history, only biography"?

   Source: _____
   Answer: _____
   _____

From *Cruising Through Research.* © 1998 John D. Volkman. (800) 237-6124.

English Reference Questions

Name: _____

Teacher: _____ Period: _____

Sheet 33

1. English writer Daniel Defoe, son of a tallow dealer and creator of *Robinson Crusoe*, added what to his name in the hope of seeming more well bred?

   Source: _____
   Answer: _____
   _____

2. Many people think that Flannery O'Connor, a short story writer and novelist of the 1950s, was a man. When she was five, she became a national celebrity. How?

   Source: _____
   Answer: _____
   _____

3. Ellery Queen is best known as a detective story writer, but that name is a pseudonym for two men who secretly wrote as one. Name the two men.

   Source: _____
   Answer: _____
   _____

4. In *Jason and the Golden Fleece*, Pelias was warned about a stranger he would meet. What was to be the "identifying mark" of the stranger?

   Source: _____
   Answer: _____
   _____

5. Izanagi and his sister Izanami are the creators of the world, according to Japanese mythology. Inzanami is the primeval mother of what?

   Source: _____
   Answer: _____
   _____

6. *Shangri-la* is a term used today to describe a perfect place. The original Shangri-La was in a novel. Name the novel's author and title.

   Source: _____
   Answer: _____
   _____

7. "He could whip his weight in wildcats" is a quote from a western ballad with a character named Hoover in it. What is Hoover's nickname?

   Source: _____
   Answer: _____
   _____

From *Cruising Through Research* © 1998 John D. Volkman. (800) 237-6124.

94 / Excursion 2: English Reference Books

English Reference Questions

Name: _____

Teacher: _____ Period: _____

Sheet 34

1. Denise Levertov is a famous contemporary American poet. Where was she born, and what did she do during World War II?

   Source: _____
   Answer: _____
   _____

2. Even though Langston Hughes's poetry was concerned with depicting Black America, his poems were translated into six different languages. What are they?

   Source: _____
   Answer: _____
   _____

3. "The Rubaíyát of Omar Khayyám" is a translation of lines by an 11th-century Persian poet. *Rubaíyát* is a literary term. What does it mean?

   Source: _____
   Answer: _____
   _____

4. What were the first names of Dr. Jekyll and Mr. Hyde in the book by Robert Louis Stevenson?

   Source: _____
   Answer: _____
   _____

5. In Hottentot (African) mythology, Aigamuxa are occasionally encountered among the dunes. What are they?

   Source: _____
   Answer: _____
   _____

6. Golgotha is a famous place in the Bible, but its exact location is unknown. What happened there?

   Source: _____
   Answer: _____
   _____

7. "When I have fears that I may cease to be" is the first line of a famous poem. Who is the author, and what is the poem's last line?

   Source: _____
   Answer: _____
   _____

From *Cruising Through Research* © 1998 John D. Volkman. (800) 237-6124.

English Reference Questions

Name: _____

Teacher: _____ Period: _____

Sheet 35

1. James Crichton won fame in England as a poet in the 16th century. He graduated from college at age 10 and was dead at age 23. How many languages did he speak?

   Source: _____
   Answer: _____
   _____

2. Although he's a modern English author, Somerset Maugham spoke another language first. What was it?

   Source: _____
   Answer: _____
   _____

3. The Latin term *carpe diem* was originally used by Horace in his *Odes*. What does it mean?

   Source: _____
   Answer: _____
   _____

4. In Shakespeare's play *Measure for Measure*, Mariana was supposed to marry Angelo. Why didn't the marriage take place?

   Source: _____
   Answer: _____
   _____

5. Ahab is the well-known captain who hunts the white whale in the novel *Moby Dick*. In the Bible, Ahab marries a famous woman. Name her.

   Source: _____
   Answer: _____
   _____

6. Zeus killed Asciepius, Apollo's son, with a thunderbolt. What did Apollo do to avenge his death?

   Source: _____
   Answer: _____
   _____

7. Samuel Hoffenstein wrote, "Babies haven't any hair; old men's heads are just as bare; between the cradle and the grave..." What is the last line?

   Source: _____
   Answer: _____
   _____

From *Cruising Through Research.* © 1998 John D. Volkman. (800) 237-6124.

96 / Excursion 2: English Reference Books

English Reference Questions

Name: _____

Teacher: _____ Period: _____

Sheet 36

1. Charlotte Brontë, author of *Jane Eyre*, fell in love with her employer while teaching in Brussels. What was she teaching, and whom did she love?

   Source: _____
   Answer: _____
   _____

2. Why was playwright Eugene O'Neill suspended from Princeton?

   Source: _____
   Answer: _____
   _____

3. What does Punch of the Punch and Judy puppet show do in angry desperation to the baby he is minding when it cries and screams and won't be soothed?

   Source: _____
   Answer: _____
   _____

4. "The Gift of the Magi" is a famous short story by O. Henry. What does the wife sell to buy her husband a watch chain for Christmas?

   Source: _____
   Answer: _____
   _____

5. The story of Hagar and her son, Ishmael, is told in the Old Testament. There is a Moslem legend about them. Where does it say they are buried?

   Source: _____
   Answer: _____
   _____

6. Euripides in Greek and Seneca in Latin wrote tragedies based on the Greek legend about Medea. What is the name of the man whom Medea loves?

   Source: _____
   Answer: _____
   _____

7. According to Voltaire, if "Crime has it heroes," what does error have?

   Source: _____
   Answer: _____
   _____

From *Cruising Through Research* © 1998 John D. Volkman. (800) 237-6124.

English Reference Answers

SHEET 1
1. *20th Century Authors, 1st Supplement*
2. *British Authors Before 1800*
3. *Reader's Encyclopedia*
4. *Oxford Companion to Classical Literature*
5. *Bartlett's Familiar Quotations*
6. *Dictionary of Literary Terms*
7. *Cyclopedia of Literary Characters*

"Come on-a to My House"
"Resurrection men" stole it and sold it to Cambridge
"The Faerie Queen"
In one day; he diverted a river to run through them
A misprint
A great work, masterpiece, or production; Latin
Uncle Tom's Cabin

SHEET 2
1. *Bartlett's Familiar Quotations*
2. *Oxford Companion to American Literature*
3. *Brewer's Dictionary of Phrase and Fable*
4. *Masterplots*
5. *American Authors, 1600–1900*
6. *Dictionary of Literary Terms*
7. *Brewer's; Oxford Companion to English Literature*

"Drink and the devil had done for the rest"
"Howl"
T. D. Rice
$28.00
$4.00; *Atlantic Monthly*; 1862
10 syllables, 7 lines per stanza
151

SHEET 3
1. *Home Book of Quotations*
2. *Cyclopedia of World Authors; British Authors of the Nineteenth Century*
3. *Harper's Bible Dictionary*
4. *Twentieth Century Authors*
5. *Masterplots*
6. *Dictionary of Literary Terms*
7. *Oxford Companion to Classical Literature*

Edward Thompson
Next to the grave of his first wife in Stinsford or Dorchester
10 plagues; the death of every firstborn child
12 dogs
1,300 years
14 lines; iambic pentameter
A ball of yarn or thread

SHEET 4
1. *Home Book of Quotations*
2. *British Authors of the 19th Century*
3. *World Authors, 1950–1970*
4. *Reader's Encyclopedia*
5. *Oxford Companion to English Literature*
6. *Masterplots*
7. *Dictionary of World Mythology*

John Ray
12 children
13 years old
Holden Caulfield and Phoebe
The 15th of March, May, July, and October; the 13th of all other months
1863
A falcon

From *Cruising Through Research.* © 1998 John D. Volkman. (800) 237-6124.

98 / Excursion 2: English Reference Books

SHEET 5
1. *Bartlett's Familiar Quotations* — "The Gift Outright"
2. *American Authors, 1600–1900* — 13 brothers and sisters
3. *Oxford Companion to Classical Literature* — His wife, Alcestis
4. *Twentieth Century Authors* — 1915; medieval literature
5. *Masterplots* — 2000; Edith and Dr. Leete
6. *Harper's Bible Dictionary* — 30 pieces; he flung them in the temple
7. *Dictionary of World Mythology* — A hammer

SHEET 6
1. *Bartlett's Familiar Quotations* — A kettle
2. *Current Biography* — 15 children
3. *Twentieth Century Authors* — every
4. *Twentieth Century Authors* — 19 years old
5. *Harper's Bible Dictionary* — 40 years
6. *Masterplots* — Eight years
7. *Crowell's Handbook of Classical Mythology* — Zeus

SHEET 7
1. *Home Book of Quotations* — George Meredith
2. *World Authors, 1970–1975* — 1973; science fiction
3. *Twentieth Century Authors* — 24 years old
4. *Dictionary of Literary Terms* — Five lines and 31 syllables
5. *Who's Who in the New Testament* — 6,000 soldiers
6. *Masterplots* — That of being an honest man
7. *Oxford Companion to Classical Literature* — A spider

SHEET 8
1. *Magill's Quotations in Context* — "A seafaring man with one leg"
2. *American Authors, 1600–1900* — *Two Years Before the Mast*
3. *Twentieth Century Authors* — Five times
4. *Who's Who in the Bible* — Five times larger
5. *Dictionary of Literary Terms* — Eight pages
6. *Masterplots* — A loaf of bread
7. *Dictionary of Classical Mythology* — Alexander the Great

SHEET 9
1. *Bartlett's Familiar Quotations* — Henry David Thoreau
2. *American Authors, 1600–1900* — 20 years old
3. *Contemporary Authors, 97–100* — "Someone has to tell everyone how to act"
4. *Brewer's Dictionary of Phrase and Fable* — Beau Brummel
5. *Magill's Quotations in Context* — *A Christmas Carol*; Bob Cratchit
6. *Masterplots* — Edward
7. *Dictionary of World Mythology* — Aztec (Mexico), Toltec mythology

From *Cruising Through Research.* © 1998 John D. Volkman. (800) 237-6124.

English Reference Answers / 99

SHEET 10
1. *Bartlett's Familiar Quotations; Magill's Quotations in Context* — Moby Dick
2. *American Authors, 1600–1900* — Three wives and 15 children
3. *Who's Who in the Old Testament* — Seven years; he actually worked 14 years
4. *Twentieth Century Authors* — Nine universities
5. *Oxford Companion to American Literature* — *Pilgrim's Progress* by John Bunyan
6. *Bartlett's Familiar Quotations* — Alfred Lord Tennyson
7. *Crowell's Handbook of Classical Mythology* — Odysseus

SHEET 11
1. *British Authors of 19th Century* — 32 years old
2. *Who's Who in the Old Testament* — Eight people were saved; Noah, his three sons, and the four wives
3. *Twentieth Century Authors* — A concert pianist
4. *Magill's Quotations in Context* — A water boy; he died serving those who scorned him
5. *Masterplots* — He predicted an eclipse of the sun
6. *Dictionary of Classical Mythology* — He bathed in the river Pactolus; ears of a donkey
7. *Bartlett's Familiar Quotations* — Edgar Allan Poe

SHEET 12
1. *Harper's Bible Dictionary* — Blasphemy, idolatry, and adultery
2. *Twentieth Century Authors* — *A Daughter of Raasay*; 1902
3. *Oxford Companion to English Literature* — He drowned
4. *Oxford Dictionary of Quotations* — A. E. Housman; "A Shropshire Lad"
5. *Bartlett's Familiar Quotations* — "All the news that's fit to print"
6. *Cyclopedia of Literary Characters* — A wealthy army officer; *Anna Karenina*
7. *Dictionary of World Mythology* — Non-dead

SHEET 13
1. *American Authors, 1600–1900* — *Five Little Peppers and How They Grew*
2. *Brewer's Dictionary of Phrase and Fable* — A mighty to-do about a trifle; making a fuss about nothing
3. *Twentieth Century Authors* — Abraham Lincoln
4. *Dictionary of Literary Terms* — Words in the middle of each line rhyme
5. *Bartlett's Familiar Quotations* — "And two to bear my soul away"
6. *Masterplots* — Athos, Porthos, and Armis, with D'Artagnan
7. *Crowell's Handbook of Classical Mythology* — He built an ark

From *Cruising Through Research.* © 1998 John D. Volkman. (800) 237-6124.

100 / Excursion 2: English Reference Books

SHEET 14

1. *Current Biography; World Authors, 1970–1975*   Harvard
2. *Brewer's Dictionary of Phrase and Fable*   A star called the Dog Star
3. *World Authors, 1975–1980*   Accidents, shootings, and other violent occurrences
4. *Harper's Bible Dictionary, Who's Who in the New Testament*   John the Baptist
5. *Bartlett's Familiar Quotations*   Bible; Song of Solomon 8:6
6. *Masterplots*   Rima
7. *Oxford Companion to Classical Literature*   They were buried alive

SHEET 15

1. *Current Biography, 1985*   He changed it in eighth grade because he wanted a "stronger" name
2. *Brewer's Dictionary of Phrase and Fable*   A suckling pig
3. *American Authors, 1600–1900*   His father's strong antislavery views forced the family to move often
4. *Harper's Bible Dictionary*   Beloved
5. *Bartlett's Familiar Quotations*   He had bitten his own arm and sucked the blood; "The Ancient Mariner"
6. *Cyclopedia of Literary Characters*   Queen Elizabeth
7. *Crowell's Handbook of Classical Mythology*   By being changed into a laurel tree

SHEET 16

1. *American Authors, 1600–1900; Cyclopedia of World Authors*   She burned to death
2. *Oxford Companion to Classical Literature; Crowell's Handbook of Classical Mythology*   A centaur
3. *European Authors, 1000–1900*   19 years old
4. *Brewer's Dictionary of Phrase and Fable*   The Bible; 969 years old
5. *Magill's Quotations in Context*   British soldiers
6. *Masterplots*   The Communist Party
7. *Crowell's Handbook of Classical Mythology*   By letting himself be killed by them

SHEET 17

1. *World Authors, 1950–1970*   Philosophy
2. *Dictionary of Literary Terms*   A word or sentence read the same backward as forward; for example, civic, radar
3. *Twentieth Century Authors, First Supplement*   B.Z. am Mittab
4. *Masterplots*   Caliban; to hew wood and draw water

From *Cruising Through Research* © 1998 John D. Volkman. (800) 237-6124.

5. *Dictionary of Classical Mythology* — Castor and Pollux
6. *Bartlett's Familiar Quotations* — Samuel Johnson
7. *Reader's Encyclopedia* — Conquest, Slaughter, Famine, Death

SHEET 18
1. *British Authors Before 1800* — A drunken bully
2. *Brewer's Dictionary of Phrase and Fable* — Aesop's fable about the fox who couldn't reach the grapes
3. *Twentieth Century Authors* — Because of his failure to comprehend geometry
4. *Dictionary of Classical Mythology* — He was chained to a rock while a vulture fed on his liver
5. *Bartlett's Familiar Quotations* — Cmdr. James Lawrence
6. *Masterplots* — Constance and Lady de Winter
7. *Who's Who in the Old Testament* — David and Bathsheba

SHEET 19
1. *Twentieth Century Authors, First Supplement; Cyclopedia of World Authors* — Aeronautical engineering
2. *Cyclopedia of Literary Characters* — He is the infant son of Hector; he is thrown from the walls and killed
3. *World Authors, 1950–1970* — He has been blind since age 3
4. *Dictionary of World Mythology* — They were chopped off by her father
5. *Reader's Encyclopedia* — *David Copperfield*
6. *Masterplots, Reader's Encyclopedia* — Yossarian
7. *Home Book of Quotations* — Poet John Dryden

SHEET 20
1. *Oxford Companion to English Literature* — Alexander Selkirk
2. *Dictionary of Literary Terms* — Arithmetic, music, geometry, and astronomy
3. *Twentieth Century Authors* — Blindness
4. *Oxford Companion to Classical Literature* — Continence (no sex)
5. *Magill's Quotations in Context* — Dylan Thomas; "After the first death, there is no other"
6. *Who's Who in the Old Testament* — Her attendants hurled her from a window
7. *Masterplots* — She threw herself under a train

SHEET 21
1. *World Authors, 1975–1980* — Because of anti-Semitism
2. *American Authors, 1600–1900* — He never wrote any of them down, but could recall any of them at will
3. *Oxford Companion to American Literature* — Boneless, quasi-human figures

102 / Excursion 2: English Reference Books

4. *Dictionary of Classical Mythology*	He had to continually roll a stone up a hill
5. *Bartlett's Familiar Quotations*	Mark Twain
6. *Who's Who in the Old Testament*	Eliphaz, Bildad, and Zophar
7. *Cyclopedia of Literary Characters*	Esmeralda; she is hanged

SHEETS 22

1. *American Authors, 1600–1900*	*Atlantic Monthly*
2. *Dictionary of Literary Terms*	Blood, phlegm, yellow bile, and black bile
3. *Twentieth Century Authors*	Brazil
4. *Oxford Companion to Classical Literature*	Bellerophon
5. *Home Book of Quotations*	Edward Bulwer-Lytton
6. *Who's Who in the Old Testament*	Esau
7. *Masterplots*	Figaro

SHEETS 23

1. *American Authors, 1600–1900*	"Barbara Frietchie"
2. *Twentieth Century Authors*	Bulldog Drummond
3. *Dictionary of Literary Terms*	For example, *buzz, crack, sizzle*
4. *Dictionary of Classical Mythology*	Daedalus
5. *Bartlett's Familiar Quotations*	England; described by Shakespeare in *Richard II*
6. *Masterplots*	George Emerson
7. *Harper's Bible Dictionary*	The Tigris and Euphrates

SHEET 24

1. *Dictionary of Literary Terms*	Horace's Ode I, xi
2. *Twentieth Century Authors*	Canned beans, coffee, and cigarettes
3. *Dictionary of Classical Mythology; Oxford Companion to Classical Literature*	Daedalus (King Minos had it built)
4. *Home Book of Quotations*	R. M. Milnes
5. *Masterplots*	Fritz, Ernst, Jack, and Francis
6. *Who's Who in the Old Testament; Harper's Bible Dictionary*	He divorced her or removed her from office
7. *World Authors, 1970–1975*	Detroit, Michigan

SHEET 25

1. *World Authors, 1950–1970*	English
2. *Who's Who in Greek and Roman Mythology; Crowell's Handbook of Classical Mythology*	Myrrh
3. *Twentieth Century Authors, First Supplement*	Clive Hamilton
4. *Dictionary of World Mythology*	Deadly arrows, huge mace, incurable diseases, and a boar

English Reference Answers / 103

5. *Bartlett's Familiar Quotations* — Francis Bacon
6. *Masterplots* — Gabriel; she finds him dying in an almshouse after she becomes a nun
7. *Brewer's Dictionary of Phrase and Fable* — Henry Wadsworth Longfellow in "Tales of a Wayside Inn"

SHEET 26
1. *Twentieth Century Authors, First Supplement; Cyclopedia of World Authors* — Budapest, Hungary
2. *Twentieth Century Authors* — Colón, Panama
3. *Dictionary of Literary Terms* — Blank
4. *Dictionary of Classical Mythology* — Demeter
5. *Magill's Quotations in Context* — "The Ballad of Dead Ladies" by Francois Villon
6. *Masterplots* — Gawain did not tell the host about the girdle
7. *Harper's Bible Dictionary* — A whip of cords and thongs; used to punish

SHEET 27
1. *European Authors, 1000–1900* — In the chest and left hand
2. *Twentieth Century Authors* — Commodore Oliver Perry
3. *Bartlett's Familiar Quotations* — Henry Wadsworth Longfellow
4. *Oxford Companion to Classical Literature* — Double-headed axe
5. *Masterplots* — Geneva, Switzerland
6. *Cyclopedia of Literary Characters* — Guide
7. *Oxford Dictionary of Quotations* — Honey and plenty of money

SHEET 28
1. *American Authors, 1600–1900* — Chevalier and Diva
2. *World Authors, 1985–1990* — Sacred Heart
3. *Reader's Encyclopedia* — Lords Spiritual, Lords Temporal, and the Commons
4. *Dictionary of Classical Mythology* — The goddess of retributive justice or vengeance
5. *Masterplots* — Guardians, auxiliaries, workers; rational, spirited, appetite
6. *Cyclopedia of Literary Characters* — John Henry West and Bernice Sadie Brown
7. *Bartlett's Familiar Quotations* — I Corinthians 15:55

SHEET 29
1. *Twentieth Century Authors, First Supplement* — His arrest for treason for supporting the Nazis and Fascists
2. *Twentieth Century Authors* — Croaghpatrick

From *Cruising Through Research.* © 1998 John D. Volkman. (800) 237-6124.

104 / Excursion 2: English Reference Books

3. *Cyclopedia of Literary Characters*	He hangs himself in a concentration camp
4. *Crowell's Handbook of Classical Mythology*	The *Argo*
5. *Who's Who in the Old Testament*	His half-brother Amnon
6. *Bartlett's Familiar Quotations*	Emma Lazarus
7. *Reader's Encyclopedia*	The kingfisher

SHEET 30

1. *Cyclopedia of World Authors*	Vivian Grey
2. *Twentieth Century Authors*	Embezzlement from a bank when he worked as a teller
3. *American Authors, 1600–1900*	He wrote a defense for the California bandit Joaquin Murietta
4. *Masterplots*	He faints
5. *Oxford Companion to Classical Literature*	Odysseus; they forget home and stay in Lotus-Land
6. *Oxford Companion to English Literature*	John Gay
7. *Bartlett's Familiar Quotations*	Isaac Watts; Psalm 98

SHEET 31

1. *American Authors, 1600–1900*	Corset making
2. *World Authors, 1950–1970*	*Battle Cry*
3. *Dictionary of Literary Terms*	Five; aabba; a county in Ireland
4. *Masterplots*	His boots
5. *Who's Who in Greek & Roman*	He looked back at her while leading her out of Hades
6. *Brewer's Dictionary of Phrase and Fable*	Lion's Prerogative, superior courage, female/cubs, no dispute
7. *Home Book of Quotations*	*The Critic*

SHEET 32

1. *World Authors, 1950–1970*	David John Moore Cornwell
2. *Dictionary of Literary Terms*	Five, seven, and then five again
3. *Oxford Companion to American Literature*	Frank Lloyd Wright
4. *Masterplots*	He was anonymously buying on the bull side of the stock market
5. *Crowell's Handbook of Classical Mythology*	Hera
6. *Cyclopedia of Literary Characters*	James Fenimore Cooper
7. *Bartlett's Familiar Quotations*	Ralph Waldo Emerson

SHEET 33

1. *British Authors Before 1800; Reader's Encyclopedia*	De
2. *World Authors, 1950–1970*	She owned a bantam chicken who walked backwards

3. *Twentieth Century Authors* — Frederic Danney and Manfred B. Lee
4. *Masterplots* — He would be wearing only one sandal
5. *Dictionary of World Mythology* — Shinto
6. *Reader's Encyclopedia* — James Hilton; *Lost Horizon*
7. *Magill's Quotations in Context* — Three-fingered

SHEET 34
1. *World Authors, 1950–1970* — England; she was a nurse
2. *Twentieth Century Authors* — French, German, Spanish, Russian, Yiddish, and Czech
3. *Dictionary of Literary Terms* — Quatrain (four-line stanza)
4. *Cyclopedia of Literary Characters* — Henry Jekyll and Edward Hyde
5. *Dictionary of World Mythology* — Strange, human-eating monsters
6. *Harper's Bible Dictionary* — Jesus was crucified
7. *Bartlett's Familiar Quotations* — John Keats; "Till love and fame to nothingness do sink"

SHEET 35
1. *British Authors Before 1800* — 11 languages
2. *Twentieth Century Authors* — French
3. *Reader's Encyclopedia* — Seize the day
4. *Masterplots* — Her dowry was lost at sea
5. *Who's Who in the Old Testament* — Jezebel
6. *Oxford Companion to Classical Literature* — He killed the Cyclops who made the thunderbolt
7. *Bartlett's Familiar Quotations* — "Lies a haircut and a shave"

SHEET 36
1. *British Authors of 19th Century* — English; M. Heger
2. *Twentieth Century Authors* — He committed a youthful misdemeanor
3. *Reader's Encyclopedia* — He kills it
4. *Oxford Companion to American Literature* — Her hair
5. *Who's Who in the Old Testament* — Ka'aba in Mecca
6. *Oxford Companion to Classical Literature; Crowell's Handbook of Classical Mythology* — Jason
7. *Home Book of Quotations* — Martyrs

Excursion 3
Patriot Passage

Patriot Passage Instructions

Destination: Term-Paper Tactics

The Patriot Passage is preparation for writing term papers. Once students have successfully completed this assignment, they will find future research projects to be "smooth sailing." They have already packed their bags with some reference tools (Excursion 1); now they are ready to set sail in uncharted water. There is no need to send out an SOS . . . the water is passable. As the pilot, you will be steering the students through research obstacles by teaching them the following skills: finding and recording reference sources, note-taking, outlining, being creative, using parenthetical notes, making a bibliography, writing a rough draft, and using a computer to make a final draft (two to three pages).

Cargo

Appropriate reference books (See suggested list on pp. 111–12)
Overhead projector
Author strips (fig. 3.1 on p. 113)
Copies of the assignment (fig. 3.2 on p. 114–15)
Overheads of the assignment and all examples (figs. 3.2, 3.5–3.13 on pp. 114–15, 118–28; can be enlarged 25%)
Copies of "Research Notes" form and "Your Future" note form (figs. 3.3 and 3.4 on pp. 116–17)
Copies of the examples for each student

Preparation

1. Copy the names of the "Patriot Passage Authors" (fig. 3.1) onto card stock or construction paper and cut into individual strips. To make them last, laminate the paper before cutting. Keep them in an envelope or similar container.

2. Prepare enough copies of the "Invitation for a Two-Week Cruise" (fig. 3.2) so that each student can have a copy. In the CAPTAIN'S LOG of the Invitation, put down the Dewey Decimal numbers of the appropriate reference books to remind the students of their location.

3. Make overhead transparencies of all the instructions and examples. Put them in clear plastic covers and keep them in a binder to help preserve and organize them as you use them to present the lesson.

4. Prepare enough copies of the note forms so that each student will have one "Your Future" note form (fig. 3.3) and four "Research Notes" forms (fig. 3.4).

5. Make a packet for each student that includes a copy of all of the example notes, the letter, the outline, and the bibliography (figs. 3.5 to 3.13).

6. Have a stack of "Research Notes" forms (fig. 3.4) available for students to use as they need them.

Navigation Instructions

Day 1

1. Pass out a copy of figure 3.2 to each student. Also give each student one of the author strips, a "Your Future" note form (fig. 3.3), four "Research Notes" forms (fig. 3.4), and the example packet. To encourage students not to lose their packets, I charge for replacement copies.

2. Explain to the students the premise of the assignment and then have them write down the name of their author from their author strip on the line in the second paragraph of their "Invitation for a Two-Week Cruise" handout. State that the students will be using four reference books as well as their imagination to complete this assignment.

3. Tell them to first of all be thinking about what they might be doing in the future and to jot their ideas down on the "Your Future" note form as they think of them. They can also include information about the futures of their classmates (gossip). Explain the possible topics, using a sample completed form (fig. 3.5) on an overhead projector.

4. Spell out the point values of the various parts of the assignment as shown on the back of the invitation. Emphasize the importance of their using the "Research Notes" forms in their research and in compiling their bibliography.

5. Tell the students that the first thing they need to do is to pick a port of call. Show them where your atlases are if they need help in selecting a port. Then show them the geography reference books from which they are to choose a port of call.

6. Show the students how to find the necessary bibliographic information from the title page and verso. Indicate how to write this information down on the "Research Notes" form, pointing out that it is set up in the same order as information will appear in their actual bibliography. It is necessary to mention that the AUTHOR refers to the author of the book being used, not the author who is sponsoring the cruise. This author's name will be put on the SUBJECT line on tomorrow's "Research Notes" form. Students should also jot down the call number of the book used so that it will be easier to find for further research.

7. Use your overhead example of a Research Note (fig. 3.6) to explain to the students how to write down five to eight facts about the port of call. Explain to them that they are to write phrases, not sentences. Remind them to be selective in choosing intriguing facts that they can use in the letter. Such things as tourist sites, entertainment, description of the people, and historic events are possible topics to consider.

8. Now display on the overhead and read that portion of the letter (fig. 3.7) that describes the future and the port of call. Then it is time to start the research. (Remind the students that it is their responsibility to bring the cruise invitation, their notepapers, and example packet to class each day.)

Day 2

1. Ask the students what a quotation is. Point out that the library has many books of just quotations in the reference section. After pointing out their location, explain how to use the quotation books. Students can use any quotations from these books, keeping in mind that they will need to use them in the letter. Point out on your overhead transparency of the quotation notes (fig. 3.8) how to write down the quote and the author of it, as well as the proper bibliographic information.

2. Point out the location of the author reference books in your school library. The students are to use one of these books to find an article on their author. Use the overhead transparency illustrated in figure 3.9 to explain that the students are to write down five to eight interesting facts about the author on their copy of the "Research Notes" form. Emphasize "interesting" as opposed to "when born," "what college attended," or similar dry facts. They should include such things as type of writer, what kind of person, titles of the author's works, and intriguing anecdotes.

3. Again, show the corresponding portions of the letter (fig. 3.7) on the overhead, pointing out how the quote is creatively worked into the letter. Mention how the factual information on the author is combined with imaginative ideas to make the letter personal and creative. Then release them to do their research.

Day 3

1. Today the students have a choice of doing research on either a disease or an animal. In researching a disease, the students are to use your medical reference books and select a disease that they have never heard of and write down five to eight facts about it, including its causes, symptoms, and treatment. Illustrate on the overhead, using figure 3.10.

2. In researching an exotic pet, the students are to use your wildlife reference books, select an animal that is not normally considered a pet, and write down five to eight facts about it, including its appearance, habitat, and diet. (I like to mention creative uses of exotic pets such as maintaining piranhas in the swimming pool to keep the neighborhood kids out.) Illustrate on the overhead, using figure 3.11.

3. Use the overhead transparency of the letter (fig. 3.7) to show how these facts were creatively woven into the letter. (When the students do their research, notice how they love to browse the medical and animal books for weird and fun pictures and facts.)

Day 4

1. Once the students have completed their research, have them organize their information in an outline. Show the outline (fig. 3.12) on the overhead and briefly explain that the primary purpose of the outline is to help them better organize their research.

2. This is the last day for library research during class time. Students will be writing the letter as homework and in class. Obtain from the teacher a due date or time line for completion of the assignment and share this with the students.

3. Point out items 3 and 4 in the Research Requirements section of the "Invitation for Two-Week Cruise." These will be inserted after the paper is written. Briefly explain that item 3 is called a "parenthetical note" and is now preferred in most colleges over the use of footnotes. The title may be shortened if it is a very long one.

4. Item 4 will assist the teacher and student in assuring that all four reference items are included in the letter.

5. Display the completed bibliography (fig. 3.13) on the overhead projector, reminding the students that they are to have written down all the required information on "Research Notes" forms. The teacher can go over the bibliography in more detail during class time.

Automatic Pilot

1. Your instructing is now over. The students will finish their research and write their letters. The teacher will grade the papers. However, do read some of the best papers after they are graded to see how the students have done and how the lesson can be improved.

2. Suggest to the teachers that they read over the students' rough drafts before the final draft is written or that they may want to use peer editing where the students read each others' papers and make suggestions.

3. Teachers should insist that the final draft be typed and printed out using a computer so they can work on proper formatting with the students.

Drydock

Students who miss the opening presentation are given all of the items listed in number 1 on Day 1. Retain about five or six author strips in a separate envelope to draw names for these absentees. By giving them the example packet, your explanation of the assignment can be minimized.

Additional Naval Stores

1. The following bibliography is a list of sources that I use and is provided for your use in setting up the assignment. Your library should have the same or similar sources. You may or may not provide a similar list to the students. (The local Dewey Decimal numbers in the CAPTAIN'S LOG of the Invitation is all I provide to remind the students of the location of the reference books.)

2. The four topic areas (port of call, quotation, author, and disease/animal) can also be researched using electronic sources. For example, the port of call could be researched in *Encarta*, *Information Finder*, or the *SIRS Government Reporter* (which includes *Background Notes*). The quotations could be found in *Correct Quotes* or *Microsoft Bookshelf*. The author could be looked up in Gale's *Discovering Authors*. The disease could be located in *Family Doctor* or *Biology Digest*; the animal on a CD-ROM such as National Geographic's *Mammals*.

Patriot Passage Bibliography

(Editor's Note: Dates are not included on this list because of the many editions and the annual editions that exist for many reference books.)

Port of Call

Countries of the World and Their Leader Yearbook. Detroit: Gale Research.

Encyclopedia of World Geography. New York: Marshall Cavendish.

Hubbard, Monica M., and Beverly Baier, eds. *Cities of the World*. Detroit: Gale Research.

Lands and Peoples. Danbury, CT: Grolier.

Worldmark Encyclopedia of the Nations. Detroit: Gale Research.

112 / Excursion 3: Patriot Passage

Quotation

Bartlett, John. *Familiar Quotations*. Boston: Little, Brown.

Partington, Angela, ed. *The Oxford Dictionary of Quotations*. New York: Oxford University Press.

Stevenson, Burton, ed. *The Home Book of Quotations*. New York: Dodd, Mead.

Author

Collier, Laurie, and Joyce Nakamura, eds. *Major Authors and Illustrators for Children and Young Adults*. Detroit: Gale Research.

Garrett, Agnes, and Helga P. McCue, eds. *Authors and Artists for Young Adults*. Detroit: Gale Research.

Great Writers of the English Language. New York: Marshall Cavendish.

Junior Authors and Illustrators. New York: H. W. Wilson.

Magill, Frank N., ed. *Cyclopedia of World Authors*. Englewood Cliffs, NJ: Salem Press.

Wilson Author Series. New York: H. W. Wilson.
  American Authors, 1600–1900.
  British Authors Before 1800.
  British Authors of the Nineteenth Century.
  European Authors, 1000–1900.
  Twentieth Century Authors.
  Twentieth Century Authors: First Supplement.
  World Authors, 1950–1970.
  World Authors, 1970–1975.
  World Authors, 1975–1980.
  World Authors, 1980–1985.
  World Authors, 1985–1990.

Disease

Fishbein's Illustrated Medical and Health Encyclopedia. Westport, CT: H. S. Stuttman.

Magill's Medical Guide: Health and Illness. Englewood Cliffs, NJ: Salem Press.

Marshall Cavendish Encyclopedia of Family Health. New York: Marshall Cavendish.

Marshall Cavendish Encyclopedia of Health. New York: Marshall Cavendish.

Animal

Encyclopedia of the Animal World. Sydney, Australia: Bay Books.

Encyclopedia of the Animal World. New York: Facts On File.

Marshall Cavendish International Wildlife Encyclopedia. New York: Marshall Cavendish.

Patriot Passage Authors

Ray Bradbury	Charlotte Brontë	Emily Brontë
Gwendolyn Brooks	Alice Childress	Sandra Cisneros
Stephen Crane	Michael Crichton	Charles Dickens
Lois Duncan	Paula Fox	Robert Frost
Lynn Hall	Virginia Hamilton	Lorraine Hansberry
S. E. Hinton	Langston Hughes	Maxine Hong Kingston
Dean Koontz	Madeleine L'Engle	Philip Levine
C. S. Lewis	Norma Fox Mazer	Gloria Miklowitz
Toni Morrison	Farley Mowat	Walter Dean Myers
Ogden Nash	Scott O'Dell	George Orwell
Gary Paulsen	Richard Peck	Edgar Allen Poe
Leo Politi	William Saroyan	William Sleator
Gary Soto	John Steinbeck	Todd Strasser
Amy Tan	Mildred Taylor	Mark Twain
Kurt Vonnegut	H. G. Wells	Oscar Wilde
Richard Wright	Paul Zindel	

From *Cruising Through Research.* © 1998 John D. Volkman. (800) 237-6124.

Fig. 3.1. Copy this page onto card stock, laminate, then cut into individual strips (one name per strip) to hand out to students.

Patriot Passage II

June 1, 20_____

Invitation for a Two-Week Cruise

LAUNCH
Let your imagination sail. It is ten years from now. You, as a past member of this English class, were invited to a ten-year reunion aboard a luxury cruise ship. The ship left from New York Harbor and your cruise lasted 14 days.

The famous author _____ paid all of your travel expenses because of the enduring contribution made to literature by your English class.

After you returned from the cruise, you realized that one of your best friends was not on it. To reestablish contact with this classmate, you decide to write a letter relating specific details about this exciting cruise and also about your personal life.

CAPTAIN'S LOG (Reference Books)
Using the library reference books, describe the following items:
1. Your port of call, including information about it and what you saw there
2. A quotation that has meaning to you
3. Interesting facts about the famous author who paid your expenses for the cruise
4. The disease, illness, or injury from which you, your spouse, or other relative or passenger just recovered **or** an anecdote or story about your exotic pet

PASSENGER'S DIARY
A. Your future home, education, career, family and other personal items
B. Gossip or tidbits about other passengers (members of your class)

CREW'S SPECIAL ORDERS (Research Requirements)
1. You must use at least four different sources and have a "Research Notes" form for each of the requirements listed in the CAPTAIN'S LOG.
2. You must jot down your ideas about the future and gossip on the "Your Future" handout.
3. In the body of your paper, in parentheses, include your reference. For instance you may write, "Michael Jordan played for North Carolina" (*Current Biography*).
4. In the margin, put the number of the specific requirement from the CAPTAIN'S LOG that you are fulfilling.

From *Cruising Through Research.* © 1998 John D. Volkman. (800) 237-6124.

Fig. 3.2. Provide a copy to each student at the start of this excursion.

5. Be sure to include a bibliography indicating the sources you used. In citing your sources, use correct bibliographic form, as shown in the examples below. Indent the second line five spaces. (Many reference books have no author, so just start with the title in those cases.) Arrange the entries alphabetically by author or (if there is no author) by title.

For a book with one author:
Bartlett, John. *Familiar Quotations.* Boston: Little, Brown and Co., 1968.

For a book that is edited:
Kunitz, Stanley J., ed. *American Authors, 1600–1900.* New York: H. W. Wilson, 1938.

For an encyclopedia:
"Flamingo." *The Marshall Cavendish International Wildlife Encyclopedia.* New York: Marshall Cavendish, 1989.

CARGO (hand in the following)
1. Completed "Your Future" note form and "Research Notes" forms
2. Outline
3. Rough draft
4. Final copy of the letter
5. Bibliography

BILL OF LADING (points assigned)

1. Completed "Your Future" note form	5 pts.	_____
2. Four completed "Research Notes" forms	20 pts.	_____
3. Outline	5 pts.	_____
4. Rough draft	10 pts.	_____
5. Final draft	20 pts.	_____
6. Bibliography	5 pts.	_____
Total	65 pts.	_____

Grading Scale		
	65.0–58.5	A
	58.4–52	B
	51.9–45.5	C
	45.4–39	D
	38.9–0	F

From *Cruising Through Research.* © 1998 John D. Volkman. (800) 237-6124.

116 / Excursion 3: Patriot Passage

NAME:_____

YOUR FUTURE

Possible Topics:
- Where you live
- Education, job, career
- Marriage, kids, personal honors, accomplishments
- Classmate gossip, people you've met

IDEAS: _____

_____

_____

_____

_____

_____

_____

NAME:_____

YOUR FUTURE

Possible Topics:
- Where you live
- Education, job, career
- Marriage, kids, personal honors, accomplishments
- Classmate gossip, people you've met

IDEAS: _____

_____

_____

_____

_____

_____

_____

From *Cruising Through Research.* © 1998 John D. Volkman. (800) 237-6124.

Fig. 3.3. Photocopy, cut sheet in half, and distribute one copy to each student.

Research Notes / 117

RESEARCH NOTES

YOUR NAME: _____

CALL NUMBER
_____
_____
_____
_____

_____
AUTHOR (OR EDITOR)

_____.
TITLE

_____ : _____ , _____ .
PLACE   PUBLISHER   YEAR PUBLISHED

SUBJECT or TOPIC: _____ PAGES USED: _____

NOTES: _____
_____
_____
_____
_____
_____

RESEARCH NOTES

YOUR NAME: _____

CALL NUMBER
_____
_____
_____
_____

_____
AUTHOR (OR EDITOR)

_____.
TITLE

_____ : _____ , _____ .
PLACE   PUBLISHER   YEAR PUBLISHED

SUBJECT or TOPIC: _____ PAGES USED: _____

NOTES: _____
_____
_____
_____
_____
_____

From *Cruising Through Research*. © 1998 John D. Volkman. (800) 237-6124.

Fig. 3.4. Photocopy, enlarging 25%, cut in half, and distribute several to each student.

NAME:_____

YOUR FUTURE

Possible Topics:
- Where you live
- Education, job, career
- Marriage, kids, personal honors, accomplishments
- Classmate gossip, people you've met

IDEAS: *Houston Univ. of Texas (Austin)*

Met wife in college, 1 boy

Johnson Space Center, Rocket Scientist

Met Astronauts

NASA award for rocket to Venus

From *Cruising Through Research*. © 1998 John D. Volkman. (800) 237-6124.

Fig. 3.5. Create an overhead transparency to use in instructing the students how to fill out the Your Future form.

SAMPLE RESEARCH NOTES: Port of Call

YOUR NAME: _John Smith_

AUTHOR (OR EDITOR): _Young, Margaret_

TITLE: _Cities of the World_

CALL NUMBER: _____

PLACE: _Detroit_ : PUBLISHER: _Gale_ , YEAR PUBLISHED: _1987_

SUBJECT or TOPIC: _Hong Kong_   PAGES USED: _163-177_

NOTES: _Premiere commercial & financial market in Asia_

Victoria Peak—1825 ft.—scenic overlook—cable car

Beaches—crowded, small and polluted

Population—more than 6M, 98% Chinese

2 main religions: Buddhism & Taoism, 10% Christian

Hot & humid, monsoons in summer & winter

99% humidity some days

Space museum in Kowloon

American women—no ready-made clothes—sizes too small

From *Cruising Through Research*. © 1998 John D. Volkman. (800) 237-6124.

Fig. 3.6. Create an overhead transparency to use in instructing the students how to take notes on the port of call.

August 5, 2007

Dear Jerome,

How are you doing? I haven't seen you since you came to my graduation from the University of Texas down in Austin. You met my girlfriend then. We are now married and have a two-year-old son. Remember how everyone used to kid me about "being a rocket scientist" because I did so well in physics and chemistry? Well, believe it or not, I now work at the Johnson Space Center in Houston doing that very thing. In fact, I received an award from NASA for helping to design the rocket that just went to Venus. Do you remember how good Art was at drawing our pictures? Well, he now has a cartoon series called Famous Faces and is syndicated in more than 100 newspapers. Come on down sometime and see me; I'll tell you the *whole* story about Denise in Dallas.

[1] By the way, we sure missed you on the trip to Hong Kong. This city of more than six million people is sure a lot different from Fresno. It is one of the premiere commercial and financial markeplaces in Asia—we certainly did our share of shopping! Remember how we thought Fresno was hot? Well, the humidity in Hong Kong was 99% most of the time, so we felt like we were in a sauna. Going to the beaches didn't even help much because they are crowded, small, and polluted. We got caught in one of the monsoons which hit during the summer and got soaked. But when some of the girls wanted to buy ready-made clothes, they had a hard time finding them because most of the sizes were too small. My favorite part of the whole trip was the spectacular view of the city from the top of Victoria Peak. Just like in San Francisco, we got to ride a cable car to the top of this 1,825-foot peak (*Cities of the World*).

From *Cruising Through Research.* © 1998 John D. Volkman. (800) 237-6124.

Fig. 3.7. Sample letter. Create an overhead transparency to use in instructing the students how to write the research-based letter.

[2] Do you remember Sally Goodman? She was on the trip. When we went to the Space Museum in Kowloon, Hong Kong, we all had to resist the temptation to call her by her class nickname: Space Cadet. She's still a little different, but I remembered what T. H. Thompson once said: "Be kind. Remember everyone you meet is fighting a hard battle" (*Familiar Quotations*). I think we've all matured during the last 10 years.

[3] As one who has always loved the sea, I was excited to meet Jack London, the author who sponsored our trip. When he was growing up in Oakland, California, he was a pirate for awhile and also loved to read about travel and sea voyages. One of his most famous books was called *Sea Wolf*. I stayed up late one evening getting to know him, and he told me that he never met his father and was raised in poverty. But at the age of 10 he discovered the Oakland Public Library and the world of books. He eventually came to be known as "the highest-paid, best known, and most popular writer in the world." There was a real mystery when he died. The death was attributed to natural causes, but written on a paper on his nightstand was the lethal dose of morphine, leading to the possibility of suicide (*Twentieth Century Authors*).

[4] Unfortunately, I was bitten by a mosquito while in Africa. No big deal, you might think. But you would be wrong, because in Africa, the mosquitoes carry a virus called malaria which means "bad air." In Africa alone it kills an estimated 1 million children under the age of 14 each year. Obviously I didn't die, but I had headaches, sweating, shivering, and pains in my arms and legs. I am still taking pills to help recover from it (*Fishbein's Medical and Health Encyclopedia*).

Fig. 3.7 continues on page 122.

From *Cruising Through Research.* © 1998 John D. Volkman. (800) 237-6124.

[or]

[4] On the cruise home we made a short stop in West Africa to pick up my newest pet—a Chevrotain. It is the cutest little thing with a small head, pointed snout, and long, thin legs. I named him Rudolph because he looks sort of like a deer, but he is only a foot high. Often Chevrotains are called mouse deer, but they are related to pigs and camels. Taking care of Rudolph is really not too hard; I just have to feed him fruit and leaves (*Encyclopedia of the Animal World*).

That's just a little bit of what I've been up to. Write back and let me know what's been happening in your life. Nobody on the cruise had talked to you for a long time, and we were all curious.

Your friend,

John Smith

SAMPLE RESEARCH NOTES: Quotation

YOUR NAME: *John Smith*

Bartlett, John
AUTHOR (OR EDITOR)

Familiar Quotations
TITLE

CALL NUMBER
_____
_____
_____
_____

Boston : *Little, Brown* , *1980*
PLACE   PUBLISHER   YEAR PUBLISHED

SUBJECT or TOPIC: *Quote*   PAGES USED: *1155*

NOTES: *"Be kind. Remember everyone you meet is fighting a hard battle."*

— T. H. Thompson

From *Cruising Through Research.* © 1998 John D. Volkman. (800) 237-6124.

Fig. 3.8. Create an overhead transparency to use in instruction the student how to take notes on the quotation source.

SAMPLE RESEARCH NOTES: Author

YOUR NAME: _John Smith_

Kunitz, Stanley J.
AUTHOR (OR EDITOR)

Twentieth Century Authors
TITLE

CALL NUMBER

New York : _H. W. Wilson_ , _1942_
PLACE / PUBLISHER / YEAR PUBLISHED

SUBJECT or TOPIC: _Jack London_   PAGES USED: _843-845_

NOTES: _Illegitimate son of itinerant Irish astrologer_

Never saw his father

Raised in poverty

Discovered world of books at age 10 at Oakland Public Library

At least 11 jobs as youngster including pirate

By 1913, called "highest-paid, best known, and most popular writer in the world"

Wrote Sea Wolf, Call of the Wild, White Fang

Mystery about death—morphine—suicide?

From *Cruising Through Research.* © 1998 John D. Volkman. (800) 237-6124.

Fig. 3.9. Create an overhead transparency to use in instructing the students how to take notes on their author.

SAMPLE RESEARCH NOTES: Animal

YOUR NAME: *John Smith*

AUTHOR (OR EDITOR)

Fishbein's Medical and Health Encyclopedia
TITLE

Westford, CT : *H. S. Stuttman* , *1981*
PLACE — PUBLISHER — YEAR PUBLISHED

CALL NUMBER

SUBJECT or TOPIC: *Malaria*   PAGES USED: *1944-1946*

NOTES: *Means bad air*

In Africa, kills est. 1M children under 14 each year

Causes headaches, pains in the limbs, sweating, shivering

Treated by quinine pills to destroy parasites

Prevention drugs taken a week before arrival & for 6 weeks after departure

From *Cruising Through Research*. © 1998 John D. Volkman. (800) 237-6124.

Fig. 3.10. Create an overhead transparency to use in instructing the students how to take notes on their disease.

SAMPLE RESEARCH NOTES: Disease

YOUR NAME: *John Smith*

_____
AUTHOR (OR EDITOR)

Encyclopedia of the Animal World
TITLE

CALL NUMBER

Sydney, Aus. : *Bay Books* , *1986*
PLACE   PUBLISHER   YEAR PUBLISHED

SUBJECT or TOPIC: *Chevrotain*   PAGES USED: *380-381*

NOTES: *Tiny, deer-like*

1 foot high

Small head, pointed snout, long, thin legs

Often called Mouse Deer

Related to pigs & camels

Eat fruit & leaves

Live in swamps of West & Central Africa

From *Cruising Through Research.* © 1998 John D. Volkman. (800) 237-6124.

Fig. 3.11. Create an overhead transparency to use in instructing the students how to take notes on their animal.

Outline

I. Past few years
   A. Univ. of Texas, degree, wife and 2-year-old son
   B. Rocket Scientist, Houston
   C. NASA awards
   D. Art and Denise
II. Hong Kong
   A. Marketplace
   B. Humidity, beaches
   C. Victoria Peak
III. Quote
   A. Sally
   B. Hard battle
IV. Jack London
   A. Pirate, sea
   B. No father, poverty
   C. World of books
   D. Writer
   E. Death
V. Malaria
   A. Mosquitoes
   B. Symptoms
VI. Chevrotain
   A. Appearance
   B. Food
VII. Closing

From *Cruising Through Research.* © 1998 John D. Volkman. (800) 237-6124.

Fig. 3.12. Create an overhead transparency to use in illustrating the proper form of an outline.

Bibliography

Bartlett, John. *Familiar Quotations*. Boston: Little, Brown, 1980.

Encyclopedia of the Animal World. Sydney, Australia: Bay Books, 1986.

Fishbein's Medical and Health Encyclopedia. Westford, CT: H. S. Stuttman, 1981.

Kunitz, Stanley J. *Twentieth Century Authors*. New York: H. W. Wilson, 1942.

Young, Margaret. *Cities of the World*. Detroit: Gale Research, 1987.

From *Cruising Through Research*. © 1998 John D. Volkman. (800) 237-6124.

Fig. 3.13. Create an overhead transparency to use in illustrating the proper form of a bibliography.

Excursion 4
Queen Elizabeth Cruise

Queen Elizabeth Instructions

Destination: Term-Paper Tactics

The Queen Elizabeth assignment is preparation for writing term papers. Once students have successfully completed this assignment, they will cruise through future research. They have already stocked the hold with some reference tools (Excursions 1 and 2); now they are ready to traverse the world. Each student is the captain of his own ship, but you, as the pilot, will be steering them through research obstacles by teaching the following skills: finding and recording reference sources, note-taking, outlining, being creative, using parenthetical notes, making a bibliography, writing a rough draft, and using a computer to make a final draft. This excursion is similar to the Patriot Passage, but differs by requiring many more sources (nine to ten) and a longer letter (four to eight pages).

Cargo

Appropriate reference books (Suggested list on pp. 133–35)
Overhead projector
Author strips (fig. 4.1 on p. 136)
Copies of the assignment (fig. 4.2 on pp. 137–38)
Overheads of the assignment and all examples (figs. 4.2, 4.5–4.17 on pp. 137–38, 141–58; can be enlarged 25%)
Copies of "Research Notes" form and "Your Future" note form (figs. 4.3 and 4.4 on pp. 139–40)
Copies of the examples for each student
A map of the world for each student

Preparation

1. Copy the names of the Queen Elizabeth Authors (fig. 4.1) onto card stock or construction paper and cut into individual strips. To make them last, laminate the paper before cutting. Keep them in an envelope or similar container.

2. Prepare enough copies of the "Invitation for a Two-Week Cruise" (fig. 4.2) so that each student can have a copy. In the CAPTAIN'S LOG of the Invitation, put down the Dewey Decimal numbers of the appropriate reference books to remind the students of their location.

3. Make overhead transparencies of all the instructions and examples. Put them in clear plastic covers and keep them in a binder to help preserve and organize them as you use them to present the lesson.

4. Prepare enough copies of the note forms so that each student will have one "Your Future" note form (fig. 4.3) and nine or ten "Research Notes" forms (fig. 4.4).

5. Make a packet for each student which includes a copy of the example of each of the notes, the letter, the outline, and the bibliography (figs. 4.5 to 4.18).

6. Have a stack of "Research Notes" forms (fig. 4.4) available for students to use as they need them.

Navigation Instructions

Day 1

1. Pass out a copy of figure 4.2 to each student. Also give each student one of the authors strips, a "Your Future" note form (fig. 4.3), a "Research Notes" form (fig. 4.4), the example packet, and a world map. To encourage students not to lose their packets, I charge for replacement copies.

2. Explain to the students the premise of the assignment and then have them write down the name of their author from their author strip on the line in the second paragraph of their Invitation for a Two-Week Cruise handout. State that the students will be using seven to ten reference books as well as their imagination to complete this assignment.

3. Tell them to first of all be thinking about what they might be doing in the future and to jot their ideas down on the "Your Future" note form as they think of them. They can also include information about the futures of their classmates (gossip). Explain the possible topics, using a sample completed form (fig. 4.5) on an overhead projector.

4. Spell out the point values of the various parts of the assignment as shown on the back of the invitation. Emphasize the importance of their using the "Research Notes" forms in their research and in compiling their bibliography.

5. The students' first research topic is to find information on their famous author. Having completed the activities in Excursion 2 of this book, "Introduction to Research: English Reference Books," the students should already know where such books are located.

6. Use the overhead transparency illustrated in figure 4.6 to explain that the students are to write down five to eight interesting facts about the author on their copy of the "Research Notes" form. Show them how to write notes, not sentences. Emphasize "interesting" as opposed to "when born," "what college attended," or similar dry facts. They should include such things as type of writer, what kind of person, titles of the author's works, and intriguing anecdotes.

7. Now display on the overhead the first three paragraphs of the letter (fig. 4.7) and point out how the factual information on the author is combined with imaginative ideas to make the letter personal and creative. Then it is time for students to start their research.

Day 2

1. For this cruise, the students are to choose three to four ports of call to research. Show them where your atlases are if they need help in selecting ports. Then show them where the geography reference books are. Use the overhead transparencies of the ports (figs. 4.8, 4.9, and 4.10) to explain how to write down five to eight facts about each port of call. Remind them to be selective in choosing intriguing facts that they can use in the letter. Such things as tourist sites, entertainment, description of the people, and historic events are possible topics to consider.

2. The exotic pet element of the research will require the use of your wildlife reference books. The students are to choose an animal that is not normally considered a pet and write down five to eight facts about it, including its appearance, habitat, and diet. (I like to mention creative uses of exotic pets such as keeping a Bengal tiger to keep the dogs out of the yard.) Illustrate on the overhead, using figure 4.11.

3. Show the overhead of these parts of the letter (fig. 4.7) and point out the creativity involved, especially in the story of the lemming.

4. Students are also to draw their cruise route colorfully on a map of the world that you provide. Tell them to use one of the atlases to draw the cruise route on their maps and to copy down the bibliographic information on the "Research Notes" form. Illustrate on the overhead, using figure 4.18.

Day 3

1. Today students will use geography reference books, United States geography books, a regular encyclopedia, AAA guides, or other travel guides to research the city or country to which they have moved. (Note: If you or a friend are a AAA member, you can get state guides for free. They are a great source of information.) Use figure 4.12 to instruct students on how to take notes on their city or country.

2. As the students are already familiar with the quotation books (having used them in Excursions 2 and 3), just explain that they can use any quotation from these books that they wish. They should, however, keep in mind that they will need to use the quote in the letter. Point out on the overhead transparency (fig. 4.13) how to write down the quote and the author of it, as well as the proper bibliographic information.

3. Now show on the overhead those parts of the letter (fig. 4.7) related to the location and quotation aspects of the research. (This excerpt from a former student's letter is my favorite example and demonstrates the creativity that, ideally, will be reflected in the students' letters.)

Day 4

1. Today the students will research a famous person of interest, living or dead, using any biography reference book. Again they are to write five to eight facts about this person on a "Research Notes" form. Illustrate on the overhead using figure 4.14.

2. Next, the students are to use your medical reference books to select a disease that they have never heard of and write down five to eight facts about it, including its causes, symptoms, and treatment. Illustrate on the overhead, using figure 4.15.

Day 5

1. Once the students have completed their research, have them organize their information in an outline. Show the outline (fig. 4.16) on the overhead and briefly explain that the primary purpose of the outline is to help them better organize their research.

2. This is the last day for library research during class time. Students will be writing the letter as homework and in class. Obtain from the teacher a due date or time line for completion of the assignment and share this with the students.

3. Point out items 3 and 4 in the Research Requirements section of the "Invitation for Two-Week Cruise." These will be inserted after the paper is written. Briefly explain that item 3 is called a "parenthetical note" and is now preferred in most colleges over use of footnotes. The title may be shortened if it is a long one.

4. Item 4 will assist the teacher and student in assuring that all seven reference items are included in the letter.

5. Display the completed bibliography (fig. 4.17) on the overhead projector reminding the students that they are to have written down all the required information on "Research Notes" forms. The teacher can go over the bibliography in more detail during class time.

Automatic Pilot

1. Your instructing is now over. The students will finish their research and write their letters. The teacher will grade the papers. However, do read some of the best papers after they are graded to see how the students have done and how the lesson can be improved.

2. Suggest to the teachers that they read the students' rough drafts before the final draft is written, or that they use peer editing, where the students read each others' papers and make suggestions.

3. Teachers should insist that the final draft be typed and printed using a computer so they can work on proper formatting with the students.

Drydock

Students who miss the opening presentation are given all of the items listed in number 1 on Day 1. Retain about five or six author strips in a separate envelope to draw names for these absentees. By giving them the example packet, your explanation of the assignment can be minimized.

Additional Naval Stores

1. The following bibliography is merely a list of sources that I use and is provided for your use in setting up the assignment. Your library should have the same or similar sources. You may or may not provide a similar list to the students. (The local Dewey Decimal numbers in the CAPTAIN'S LOG of the Invitation is all I use to remind the students of the location of the reference books.)

2. The seven topic areas (author, three to four ports of call, exotic pet, present home, quotation, famous person, and disease) can also be researched using electronic sources. For example the author could be researched in Gale's *Discovering Authors*. The ports of call and home could be found in *Encarta*, *Information Finder*, or the *SIRS Government Reporter* (which includes *Background Notes*). An animal CD-ROM such as National Geographic's *Mammals* could be used for the exotic pet. A quotation could be found in *Correct Quotes* or *Microsoft Bookshelf*. Any encyclopedia CD or *Current Biography* on CD could be sources for the famous person aspect of the research. The disease could be located in *Family Doctor* or *Biology Digest*.

Queen Elizabeth Bibliography

(Editor's Note: Dates are not included on this list because of the many editions and the annual editions that exist for many reference books.)

Author

Collier, Laurie, and Joyce Nakamura, eds. *Major Authors and Illustrators for Children and Young Adults*. Detroit: Gale Research.

Garrett, Agnes, and Helga P. McCue, eds. *Authors and Artists for Young Adults.* Detroit: Gale Research.

Great Writers of the English Language. New York: Marshall Cavendish.

Junior Authors & Illustrators. New York: H. W. Wilson.

Magill, Frank N., ed. *Cyclopedia of World Authors.* Englewood Cliffs, NJ: Salem Press.

Wilson Author Series. New York: H. W. Wilson.
- *American Authors, 1600–1900.*
- *British Authors Before 1800.*
- *British Authors of the Nineteenth Century.*
- *European Authors, 1000–1900.*
- *Twentieth Century Authors.*
- *Twentieth Century Authors: First Supplement.*
- *World Authors, 1950–1970.*
- *World Authors, 1970–1975.*
- *World Authors, 1975–1980.*
- *World Authors, 1980–1985.*
- *World Authors, 1985–1990.*

Port of Call

Countries of the World and Their Leader Yearbook. Detroit: Gale Research.

Encyclopedia of World Geography. New York: Marshall Cavendish.

Hubbard, Monica M., and Beverly Baier, eds. *Cities of the World.* Detroit: Gale Research.

Lands and Peoples. Danbury, CT: Grolier.

Worldmark Encyclopedia of the Nations. Detroit: Gale Research.

Animal

Encyclopedia of the Animal World. Sydney, Australia: Bay Books.

Encyclopedia of the Animal World. New York: Facts On File.

Marshall Cavendish International Wildlife Encyclopedia. New York: Marshall Cavendish.

Home

Same books as port of call plus any regular encyclopedias, travel guides, and United States geography reference books.

Quotation

Bartlett, John. *Familiar Quotations.* Boston: Little, Brown.

Partington, Angela, ed. *The Oxford Dictionary of Quotations.* New York: Oxford University Press.

Stevenson, Burton, ed. *The Home Book of Quotations.* New York: Dodd, Mead.

Famous Person

Any reference set that includes biographies.

Disease

Fishbein's Illustrated Medical and Health Encyclopedia. Westport, CT: H. S. Stuttman.
Magill's Medical Guide: Health and Illness. Englewood Cliffs, NJ: Salem Press.
Marshall Cavendish Encyclopedia of Family Health. New York: Marshall Cavendish.
Marshall Cavendish Encyclopedia of Health. New York: Marshall Cavendish.

Queen Elizabeth Authors

Louisa May Alcott	Rudolfo Anaya	Isaac Asimov
Arna Bontemps	Charlotte Brontë	Emily Brontë
Gwendolyn Brooks	Pearl Buck	Stephen Crane
Michael Crichton	e. e. cummings	George Eliot
Robert Frost	William Golding	Thomas Hardy
Langston Hughes	Victor Hugo	Maxine Hong Kingston
Denise Leverton	Philip Levine	C. S. Lewis
Jack London	Henry Wadsworth Longfellow	Amy Lowell
Bernard Malamud	Phyllis McGinley	Edna St. Vincent Millay
Toni Morrison	Farley Mowat	Ogden Nash
George Orwell	Richard Peck	Sylvia Plath
Leo Politi	Theodore Roethke	Carl Sandburg
William Saroyan	Gary Soto	John Steinbeck
Todd Strasser	Amy Tan	Mildred Taylor
Sara Teasdale	Mark Twain	Kurt Vonnegut
H. G. Wells	Oscar Wilde	Thorton Wilder
Herman Wouk	Richard Wright	Paul Zindel

From *Cruising Through Research.* © 1998 John D. Volkman Unlimited. (800) 237-6124.

Fig. 4.1. Copy this list onto card stock, laminate, then cut into individual strips (one name per strip) to hand out to students.

Queen Elizabeth II

June 1, 20_____

Invitation for a Two-Week Cruise

LAUNCH
Let your imagination sail. It is ten years from now. You, as a past member of this English class, were invited to a ten-year reunion aboard a luxury cruise ship. The ship left from New York Harbor, and your cruise lasted 14 days.

The famous author _____ paid all of your travel expenses because of the enduring contribution made to literature by your English class.

After you returned from the cruise, you realized that one of your best friends was not on it. To reestablish contact with this classmate, you decide to write a letter relating specific details about this exciting cruise and also about your personal life.

CAPTAIN'S LOG (Reference Books)
Using the library reference books, describe the following items:
1. Interesting facts about the famous author who paid your expenses for the cruise
2. Your ports of call (three or four cities and/or countries) including information about them and what you saw there; also, indicate the ports of call and route of your trip on the map supplied
3. An anecdote or story about your exotic pet
4. Your home, that is, the city or country to which you moved (anywhere in the world), including what you like and don't like about it
5. A quotation that has meaning to you
6. Interesting facts about a famous person you met
7. The disease, illness, or injury from which you, your spouse, or other relative or passenger just recovered

PASSENGER'S DIARY
A. Your future home, education, career, family and other personal items
B. Gossip or tidbits about other passengers (members of your class)

CREW'S SPECIAL ORDERS (Research Requirements)
1. You must use at least eight different sources (only one encyclopedia), and have a "Research Notes" form for each of the requirements listed in the CAPTAIN'S LOG.
2. You must jot down your ideas about the future and gossip on the "Your Future" handout.

Fig. 4.2 continues on page 138.

From *Cruising Through Research.* © 1998 John D. Volkman Unlimited. (800) 237-6124.

Fig. 4.2. Provide a copy to each student at the start of the excursion.

3. In the body of your letter, in parentheses, include your reference. For instance you may write, "Joe Montana played for Notre Dame" (*Current Biography*).
4. In the margin, put the number of the specific requirement from the CAPTAIN'S LOG that you are fulfilling.
5. Be sure to include a bibliography indicating the sources you used. In citing your sources, use correct bibliographic form, as shown in the examples below. Indent the second line five spaces. (Many reference books have no author, so just start with the title in those cases.) Arrange the entries alphabetically by author or (if there is no author) by title.

For a book with one author:
Bartlett, John. *Familiar Quotations*. Boston: Little, Brown, 1968.

For a book that is edited:
Kunitz, Stanley J., ed. *American Authors, 1600–1900*. New York: H. W. Wilson, 1938.

For an encyclopedia:
"Flamingo." *The Marshall Cavendish International Wildlife Encyclopedia*. New York: Marshall Cavendish, 1989.

CARGO (hand in the following)
1. Completed "Your Future" note form and "Research Notes" forms
2. Outline
3. Rough draft
4. Final copy of the letter
5. Map
6. Bibliography

BILL OF LADING (points assigned)

1. Completed "Your Future" note form	5 pts.	_____
2. Nine or ten completed "Research Notes" forms	45 pts.	_____
3. Outline	10 pts.	_____
4. Rough draft	25 pts.	_____
5. Final draft	50 pts.	_____
6. Bibliography	10 pts.	_____
7. Map showing ports of call and your home	5 pts.	_____
Total	150 pts.	_____

Grading Scale
- 150–135 A
- 134–120 B
- 119–105 C
- 104–90 D
- 89–0 F

NAME:_____

YOUR FUTURE

Possible Topics:
- Where you live
- Education, job, career
- Marriage, kids, personal honors, accomplishments
- Classmate gossip, people you've met

IDEAS: _____

_____

_____

_____

_____

_____

_____

NAME:_____

YOUR FUTURE

Possible Topics:
- Where you live
- Education, job, career
- Marriage, kids, personal honors, accomplishments
- Classmate gossip, people you've met

IDEAS: _____

_____

_____

_____

_____

_____

_____

From *Cruising Through Research.* © 1998 John D. Volkman. (800) 237-6124.

Fig. 4.3. Photocopy, cut sheet in half, and distribute one copy to each student.

140 / Excursion 4: Queen Elizabeth Cruise

RESEARCH NOTES

YOUR NAME: _____

CALL NUMBER
_____
_____
_____
_____
_____

AUTOR (OR EDITOR) _____ .

TITLE _____

_____ : _____ , _____ .
PLACE   PUBLISHER   YEAR PUBLISHED

SUBJECT or TOPIC: _____ PAGES USED: _____

NOTES: _____
_____
_____
_____
_____

RESEARCH NOTES

YOUR NAME: _____

CALL NUMBER
_____
_____
_____
_____
_____

AUTHOR (OR EDITOR) _____ .

TITLE _____

_____ : _____ , _____ .
PLACE   PUBLISHER   YEAR PUBLISHED

SUBJECT or TOPIC: _____ PAGES USED: _____

NOTES: _____
_____
_____
_____

From *Cruising Through Research.* © 1998 John D. Volkman. (800) 237-6124.

Fig. 4.4. Photocopy, enlarging 25%, cut in half, and distribute several to each student.

NAME:_____

YOUR FUTURE

Possible Topics:
- Where you live
- Education, job, career
- Marriage, kids, personal honors, accomplishments
- Classmate gossip, people you've met

IDEAS: *Go to USC*

Live in L.A. area

Become actress

Use karate on mugger—get movie role

Clever names for movies

Win Oscar, Pulitzer, etc.

From *Cruising Through Research.* © 1998 John D. Volkman. (800) 237-6124.

Fig. 4.5. Create an overhead transparency to use in instructing the students how to fill out the "Your Future" form.

SAMPLE RESEARCH NOTES: Author

YOUR NAME: *Debbie Jones*

Kunitz, Stanley J.
AUTHOR (OR EDITOR)

American Authors
TITLE

CALL NUMBER

New York : *H. W. Wilson* , *1938*
PLACE   PUBLISHER   YEAR PUBLISHED

SUBJECT or TOPIC: *Edgar Allan Poe*   PAGES USED: *623-625*

NOTES: *Parents died of TB when he was 2*

Handsome, brilliant, athletic as youngster

When stepmother was dying, he got expelled

Stepfather threw him out of the house, broke up his first romance

Untrained for any profession, hypersensitive, destitute, turned to journalism

Alcoholic, one drink sent him into frenzy

Died from alcohol, half-insane at age 40

Whole existence was a "hell-life"

Wrote "The Masque of the Red Death," "The Pit and the Pendulum," and "The Raven"

From *Cruising Through Research*. © 1998 John D. Volkman. (800) 237-6124.

Fig. 4.6. Create an overhead transparency to use in instructing the students how to take notes on their author.

August 31, 2007

Dear Jennifer,

   As you have probably already figured out, the reason I am contacting you is that I noticed you weren't aboard our cruise ship. You sure missed a great trip. Can you believe Edgar Allan Poe paid for it? When he died, scientists had him frozen for future use, and 150 years later the cryogenics lab has actually defrosted him.

   When I met Mr. Poe, I was surprised to see him so vibrant. His parents had died when he was only two. Although he was handsome, brilliant, and athletic, he was not a happy child. When his stepmother was dying, Edgar refused to study and was expelled from school. He became an untrained, hypersensitive, and destitute author of unfamous poems.

[1]   Although Poe eventually became a famous author, he lived a "hell-life." Alcohol and his writing held him above insanity. In 1849 he died in an alcoholic daze. When I asked him if he was still drinking heavily, he said that he was now attending AA meetings regularly. I think his difficult childhood and the alcoholism might explain the horror found in most of his writings which included "The Masque of the Red Death," "The Pit and the Pendulum," and "The Raven" (*American Authors*).

   We left on the cruise from New York Harbor and landed first in Jamaica. Jamaica is the smallest country in the Greater Antilles in the Caribbean Sea. Its capital city is Kingston,

Fig. 4.7 continues on page 144.

From *Cruising Through Research.* © 1998 John D. Volkman. (800) 237-6124.

Fig. 4.7. Sample letter. Create an overhead transparency to use in instructing the students how to write the research-based letter.

[2] which has an extremely high crime rate. We were advised that we should never go out at night without a local escort. The area was originally a notorious pirates' lair that was destroyed by an earthquake in 1692. The next year Kingston was founded by the Spanish. In the 1940s the population skyrocketed and it has not slowed since. The highlights of our stay in Kingston were the Waterfront shopping area and the Botanical Gardens (*Cities of the World*).

[2] Our second stop was Göteborg, Sweden, which has one of the largest harbors in Europe. Marie and I were absolutely amazed at how clean the entire city is. There were beautiful summer flowers along the streets and plenty of sidewalk cafes. Some of us went on a hike through the surrounding lakes and woods, while others played "squash," a very popular sport in Sweden. That night we attended a wonderful opera, which was in Swedish (*Cities of the World*).

[2] From there we proceeded to Oslo, Norway, which is in the western part of the Scandinavian Peninsula. One third of Norway is located in the Arctic Circle, so even though it was August, the temperature didn't rise above 63°F. I wish we could have been there before July because then we could have seen the aurora borealis (*Cities of the World*).

[3] Norway *is* beautiful. We went exploring, and 2,500 feet up in the mountains we found hundreds of lemmings, which are small, furry creatures about 4 to 6 inches long. They are strange animals. The lemming population expands for a few years, and then there is a sudden crash in the numbers: Lemmings are famous for mass migration and suicide. Scientists have proven that they die because of stress, which leads to exhaustion, which causes death. Lemmings have been traditionally thought to die from drowning or because they jump off cliffs.

I found a baby lemming that seemed like it was lost, so I put it in the pocket of my coat and took it with me back to my hotel. I had to pay the room service people extra money to bring up some lichens and some moss for Matilda to eat.

From *Cruising Through Research.* © 1998 John D. Volkman. (800) 237-6124.

I wasn't sure what I would do with her after I got back home, but I sure didn't want her to take part in a mass suicide (*Illustrated Wildlife Encyclopedia*).

[4] Well, enough about the trip. It's time to catch up on ancient history, so to speak. After high school, I moved into my parents' friends' guest house in Covina, California. I went to USC with Amy; we both majored in motion picture/television, and I took a minor in English. After that, I spent much of my time suburb-hopping and looking for work. I went through my "starving actress" phase—and I moved more times in one year than most people do in a life time. I lived in Burbank, Pasadena, Watts (*that* was a frightening experience), and hard-core, downtown Hollywood. That's where my apartment was broken into. Two weeks later, I was attacked by a mugger. He didn't get very far, however, because my martial arts training finally paid off after all these years. I gave him a good, sharp elbow to the . . . well, let's just say he'll never have children (*California/Nevada Tour Book*).

Then an amazing thing happened. This man who had seen me fighting off the attacker offered me a movie role! I was stunned, needless to say. If I'd have known *that* was all I needed, I'd have beaten up someone sooner! Anyway, I was glad to get the job—no matter what the script was like. (By the way—did you see *Karate Aliens of the Mojave Desert*? I hope you have a little more class than that!) I'm a little more selective of my roles these days. In fact, just last week I turned down *Friday the 13th Part XXIV: Jason's FINALLY Dead, but His Long-Lost Cousin Is Back to Take over the Family Business*.

[5] I love to act; it's the ultimate career. But I also write plays, screenplays, and an occasional novel. In fact, I've recently been nominated for Academy Awards for Best Actress and Best Original Screenplay. (I've always wanted one of those little gold guys on my mantel!) I've already got a Tony and a Pulitzer; next I'm going for the Nobel Peace

Fig. 4.7 continues on page 146.

From *Cruising Through Research*. © 1998 John D. Volkman. (800) 237-6124.

Prize (ha ha ha). Awards are nice, and there's nothing quite like putting your name on a manuscript and having it sent back to you as a published novel. But as I always say, "I would rather be attacked than unnoticed. For the worst thing you can do to an author is to be silent as to his works." I think Samuel Johnson said that (*Familiar Quotations*).

[6] Do you remember our band days? Earlier this summer I heard James Galway, one of the most admired flute players in the world, perform at the Hollywood Palladium. I actually met and talked with him after the performance. He was born in Belfast, Northern Ireland, and began playing at age eight. Can you believe that he practices eight hours a day? I would never be able to tolerate that. We stood about eye to eye as he's only 5'4". After an automobile accident that seriously injured him, he became a devout Christian. I also got a pretty good look at his 18-karat gold flute (wow!!) (*Current Biography*).

[7] One bit of bad news before I sign off: Jan has emphysema. On the trip she was always short of breath when we had to walk anywhere, and she coughed an awful lot. When a person has emphysema, the air sacs in the lungs are damaged, and the lungs' ability to supply oxygen to the blood is progressively decreased.

Remember how Jan started smoking as a freshman, and we told her she'd wish that she hadn't? She's quit now, which helps stop the emphysema, but there is no way to repair the damage that has already been done to the lungs. That's why it is so important not to begin smoking at all (*Family Health*).

Well, I sure hope *you're* in good health. I'm anxious to hear from you, Jennifer. Maybe I'll get a chance to visit you in Brazil, but if I don't, please write.

Your friend,

Debbie Jones

SAMPLE RESEARCH NOTES: Port of Call

YOUR NAME: *Debbie Jones*

Young, Margaret
AUTHOR (OR EDITOR)

Cities of the World
TITLE

CALL NUMBER

Detroit : *Gale Research* , *1993* .
PLACE — PUBLISHER — YEAR PUBLISHED

SUBJECT or TOPIC: *Jamaica* PAGES USED: *555-578*

NOTES: *Smallest country in Greater Antilles*

Capital is Kingston-1870

Kingston-High crime rate

Notorious pirates' lair, destroyed by earthquake-1692

Spanish founded-1693

Growth rapid, slowed in 1800s by economic crises

Pop. explosion-1940s

Waterfront shopping, Botanical Gardens, Crafts Market, Univ. of West Indies

From *Cruising Through Research.* © 1998 John D. Volkman. (800) 237-6124.

Fig. 4.8. Create an overhead transparency to use in instructing the students how to take notes on the port of call.

148 / Excursion 4: Queen Elizabeth Cruise

SAMPLE RESEARCH NOTES: Port of Call

YOUR NAME: *Debbie Jones*

Young, Margaret
AUTHOR (OR EDITOR)

Cities of the World
TITLE

CALL NUMBER

Detroit : *Gale Research* , *1993*
PLACE   PUBLISHER   YEAR PUBLISHED

SUBJECT or TOPIC: *Göteborg, Sweden*   PAGES USED: *833-835*

NOTES: *large harbor*

hike in woods & lakes

clean with pretty parks

summer flowers

great beaches

"squash"-popular sport

Grand Theater, opera (all in Swedish)

sidewalk cafes

From *Cruising Through Research*. © 1998 John D. Volkman. (800) 237-6124.

Fig. 4.9. Create an overhead transparency to use in instructing the students how to take notes on the port of call.

SAMPLE RESEARCH NOTES: Port of Call

YOUR NAME: *Debbie Jones*

Young, Margaret
AUTHOR (OR EDITOR)

Cities of the World
TITLE

CALL NUMBER

Detroit : *Gale Research* , *1993* .
PLACE   PUBLISHER   YEAR PUBLISHED

SUBJECT or TOPIC: *Oslo, Norway*   PAGES USED: *633-638*

NOTES: *Western part of Scandinavian Pen.*

aurora borealis—1st half of year

1/3 in Arctic Circle, temp below 70° in summer

Beautiful mountains, rivers, fjords

Cross-country skiing is way of life

Norway became independent in 1905

From *Cruising Through Research.* © 1998 John D. Volkman. (800) 237-6124.

Fig. 4.10. Create an overhead transparency to use in instruction the students how to take notes on the port of call.

SAMPLE RESEARCH NOTES: Pet

YOUR NAME: *Debbie Jones*

AUTHOR (OR EDITOR)

TITLE: *Illustrated Wildlife Encyclopedia*

PLACE: *New York* : PUBLISHER: *Funk & Wagnalls*, YEAR PUBLISHED: *1980*

SUBJECT or TOPIC: *Lemming*   PAGES USED: *1431-1432*

CALL NUMBER

NOTES: *4-6 in. long rodent*

Thick fur, blunt muzzle, small eyes & ears

Famous for mass migration/suicide

Food is lichens, mosses & grasses

Live under the snow in the Arctic

Pop. explosion causes stress, exhaustion, death

No mass jumps off cliffs, but reckless panic marches

From *Cruising Through Research.* © 1998 John D. Volkman. (800) 237-6124.

Fig. 4.11. Create an overhead transparency to use in instructing the student how to take notes on the exotic pet.

Sample Research Notes / 151

SAMPLE RESEARCH NOTES: City or Country

YOUR NAME: *Debbie Jones*

CALL NUMBER

AUTHOR (OR EDITOR)

California/Nevada Tour Book
TITLE

Heathrow, FL : *American Automobile Assoc.*, *1994*.
PLACE — PUBLISHER — YEAR PUBLISHED

SUBJECT or TOPIC: *Los Angeles area*   PAGES USED: *90-106*

NOTES: *USC campus near Watts*

Hollywood—home to 60 movie studios

Hollywood—home of the Oscars

Concerts at Hollywood Palladium

LA pop. of 3.5M, 465 sq. miles

Collection of intermingling communities, each with own identity & character

Many sports training facilities such as martial arts

Crime, muggings—a major problem

Many aspiring actors/actresses live in the area

From *Cruising Through Research*. © 1998 John D. Volkman. (800) 237-6124.

Fig. 4.12. Create an overhead transparency to use in instructing the students how to take notes on the city or country (if foreign) in which they are living.

SAMPLE RESEARCH NOTES: Quotation

YOUR NAME: *Debbie Jones*

Bartlett, John
AUTHOR (OR EDITOR)

Familiar Quotations
TITLE

CALL NUMBER

Boston : *Little, Brown* , *1980*
PLACE   PUBLISHER   YEAR PUBLISHED

SUBJECT or TOPIC: *Quote*   PAGES USED: *356*

NOTES: *"I would rather be attacked than unnoticed. For the worst thing you can do to an author is to be silent as to his works."*

—Samuel Johnson

From *Cruising Through Research.* © 1998 John D. Volkman. (800) 237-6124.

Fig. 4.13. Create an overhead transparency to use in instructing the students how to take notes on the quotation source.

SAMPLE RESEARCH NOTES: Famous Person

YOUR NAME: *Debbie Jones*

Moritz, Charles
AUTHOR (OR EDITOR)

Current Biography
TITLE

CALL NUMBER

New York : *H. W. Wilson* , *1980*
PLACE   PUBLISHER   YEAR PUBLISHED

SUBJECT or TOPIC: *James Galway*   PAGES USED: *114-117*

NOTES: *world famous flute player*

born Belfast, Northern Ireland

practices 8 hours a day

started playing at age 8

1M LPs in Britain by 1979

18-karat gold flute

Accepted in Berlin Phil. Orch. in 1969, only English-speaking member

worked all over the world

5'4" tall

seriously injured in auto accident—became devout Christian as a result

From *Cruising Through Research*. © 1998 John D. Volkman. (800) 237-6124.

Fig. 4.14. Create an overhead transparency to use in instructing the students how to take notes on their famous person.

154 / Excursion 4: Queen Elizabeth Cruise

SAMPLE RESEARCH NOTES: Disease

YOUR NAME: _Debbie Jones_

CALL NUMBER

AUTHOR (OR EDITOR)

Marshall Cavendish Illustrated Encyclopedia of Family Health
TITLE

London : _Marshall Cavendish_ , _1986_
PLACE   PUBLISHER   YEAR PUBLISHED

SUBJECT or TOPIC: _Emphysema_   PAGES USED: _456-457_

NOTES: _Air sacs lack oxygen_

Lungs lose elasticity, blood vessels reduced

Patient easily becomes breathless, coughs a lot

Chewing, swallowing become difficult

Primary cause is smoking, also continuous dust

Cannot be cured

Use oxygen cylinders to help breathing

Stopping smoking helps, but can't reverse damage

Important not to start smoking

From *Cruising Through Research.* © 1998 John D. Volkman. (800) 237-6124.

Fig. 4.15. Create an overhead transparency to use in instructing the students how to take notes on their disease.

Outline

    I. Poe
        A. Frozen and defrosted
        B. Unhappy childhood
        C. Destitute author
        D. Problems with alcohol, AA
        E. Writings
   II. Places visited
        A. Kingston, Jamaica
            1. Crime, night
            2. Pirates' lair
            3. Population
            4. Highlights
        B. Göteborg
            1. Clean, flowers
            2. Hike, squash
            3. Opera
        C. Oslo
            1. Arctic Circle
            2. Aurora Borealis
  III. Lemmings
        A. Small, furry
        B. Cliff jumping
        C. Saving Matilda

Fig. 4.16 continues on page 156.

From *Cruising Through Research.* © 1998 John D. Volkman. (800) 237-6124.

Fig. 4.16. Create an overhead transparency to use in illustrating the proper form of an outline.

IV. My life in Hollywood
    A. "Starving actress" phase
    B. Mugger
    C. Movie roles
    D. Awards

V. Quote

VI. James Galway
    A. Flute player from Belfast
    B. Practice
    C. Auto accident, became Christian

VII. Jan with emphysema
    A. Symptoms
    B. Damage, don't start

Bibliography

Bartlett, John. *Familiar Quotations*. Boston: Little, Brown, 1980.

California/Nevada Tour Book. Heathrow, FL: American Automobile Association, 1994.

Illustrated Wildlife Encyclopedia. New York: Funk & Wagnalls, 1980.

Kunitz, Stanley J. *American Authors*. New York: H. W. Wilson, 1938.

Marshall Cavendish Illustrated Encyclopedia of Family Health. London: Marshall Cavendish, 1986.

Moritz, Charles. *Current Biography*. New York: H. W. Wilson, 1980.

World Atlas of Nations. New York: Rand McNally, 1994.

Young, Margaret. *Cities of the World*. Detroit: Gale Research, 1993.

From *Cruising Through Research*. © 1998 John D. Volkman. (800) 237-6124.

Fig. 4.17. Create an overhead transparency to use in illustrating the proper form of a bibliography.

158 / Excursion 4: Queen Elizabeth Cruise

RESEARCH NOTES

YOUR NAME: *Debbie Jones*

CALL NUMBER

_____
AUTHOR (OR EDITOR)

World Atlas of Nations
TITLE

New York : *Rand McNally* , *1994*
PLACE   PUBLISHER   YEAR PUBLISHED

SUBJECT or TOPIC: *Map*   PAGES USED: *3, 6-7, 94, 124*

NOTES: _____

_____

_____

_____

_____

_____

_____

_____

From *Cruising Through Research.* © 1998 John D. Volkman. (800) 237-6124.

Fig. 4.18. Create an overhead transparency to use in instructing the students how to write down the bibliographic information on the atlas they use for their map.

Excursion 5
World War II

World War II—Biography Instructions

As mentioned in the introduction, the World War II assignment is the prototype of my other assignments. It is still one of my favorite assignments because of the richness of sources available (we keep adding new ones each year, and since we just had the 50th anniversary of the war, there is a lot of information in periodical sources) and because the students are still fascinated with World War II, Hitler, and the Nazis.

Before embarking on this voyage into the library, review "Before You Set Sail" (pp. xiii-xv) with the classroom teacher. Then complete the following steps:

1. Schedule at least one day in the library for the class. A second or third day may follow closer to the due date.

2. If possible, have the class sit in the reference section so that you can point out the most useful reference sources. Reference books and the copy machine allow you to spread the resources around to more students.

3. Have the teacher go over the assignment with the students.

4. Briefly explain how to take notes, highlight photocopied pages, and write down the proper bibliographic information. Indicate the point value of the notes and the bibliography to the project.

5. Have available a supply of blank "Research Notes" (see p. 117) forms and encourage the students to use them or at least to copy down on paper the necessary bibliographic information.

6. Briefly mention the source list and how best to use it. (It may work best to pull some of the books most likely to be used and put them on a library cart if several classes will be using the same books.) To share the resources among classes, also have these books on reserve (overnight, three days, etc.).

7. Have the students sign up for their specific research topic.

8. Be ready to help students find information in reference books, subject specific books, collective biographies, and other sources which can require some "digging" skills.

Name _____

Teacher _____

Date _____ Period _____

World War II—Biography

World War II produced a great array of political figures, government officials, and military leaders. You are going to write a paper that explores the following person's power and his importance in the war.

LEADER _____

DUE DATE _____

ASSIGNMENT:
1. Your paper is to be at least six double-spaced, typed pages.
2. You are to address the following subjects:
   a. Personal background (family, education, upbringing, training)
   b. Description of his rise to power
   c. His ideas and philosophy
   d. His positions, title, nationality
   e. How he used his power
   f. Contributions to war or peace
   g. How he lost his power and/or died
   h. Your evaluation of his role in the war and your opinion of him as a leader

TURN IN:
1. Cover
2. Typed report
3. Collage or collection of pictures
4. At least 1 map detailing major battles in which he was involved (with an explanation in your own words) or other similar visual
5. All "Research Notes" and photocopies (highlighted and numbered, a minimum of 15)
6. Bibliography in proper form

From *Cruising Through Research*. © 1998 John D. Volkman. (800) 237-6124.

Fig. 5.1. Make a photocopy of this assignment sheet for each student.

MINIMUM RESOURCE REQUIREMENTS:
1. One *Cavendish Encyclopedia of WWII* article
2. Two other reference books
3. One other book
4. One periodical article

GRADING:

"Research Notes" forms/photocopies	20 pts.	_____
Maps/visuals	10 pts.	_____
Pictures	10 pts.	_____
Rough draft	10 pts.	_____
Written report (final copy)	40 pts.	_____
Bibliography/minimum sources	10 pts.	_____
Total	100 pts.	

Fig. 5.1 continues on page 162.

From *Cruising Through Research.* © 1998 John D. Volkman. (800) 237-6124.

WORLD WAR II REPORT— BIBLIOGRAPHY

1. Start with the following reference books.
   America in the 20th Century
   American Heritage Picture History of World War II
   Atlas of World War II
   The Marshall Cavendish Illustrated Encyclopedia of WWII (11 volumes; use index)
   Current Biography (Use index to see which year)
   Encyclopedia of Asian History
   Encyclopedia of World's Combat Aircraft
   Great Events (volume 4, 1939–1947)
   History of 20th Century (volume 5, *World War II*)
   McGraw-Hill Encyclopedia of World Biography (12 volumes)
   Rand McNally Encyclopedia of World War II
   Simon and Schuster Encyclopedia of World War II
   The Twentieth Century (volume III)
   Who Was Who in WWII (1 volume)
   The World at Arms

2. Based on your review of reference materials, choose one of the following World War II figures:

Bradley, Omar	Halsey, William	Patton, George
Chamberlin, Neville	Hirohito	Rommel, Erwin
Chiang Kai-Shek	Hitler, Adolf	Roosevelt, Franklin D.
Churchill, Winston	Hull, Cordell	Stalin, Joseph
De Gaulle, Charles	MacArthur, Douglas	Tito, Josip
Eichmann, Adolf	Marshall, George	Tojo, Hideki
Eisenhower, Dwight	Montgomery, Bernard	Truman, Harry
Goebbells, Joseph	Mussolini, Benito	Yamamoto, Isoroku
Goerring, Hermann	Nimitz, Chester	

3. Use the computer card catalog to look up topics such as:
   Your person's name
   World War II
   Presidents
   U.S. History
   Country of your person (e.g., German history book)

4. Use periodical sources from the computer network about your person or WWII:
   Newsbank for newspapers
   TOM/Infotrac (for magazines)
   Information Finder (*World Book Encyclopedia* on CD/ROM)

From *Cruising Through Research.* © 1998 John D. Volkman. (800) 237-6124.

Excursion 6

Biography

Biography Letter

In a biography letter assignment, students learn how to take notes and use their own words and creativity in writing a research paper. Students are required to integrate their information on two seemingly unrelated topics; therefore, they are prevented from plagiarizing. The concept of incorporating two seemingly unrelated topics into one writing assignment can be used to construct a lot of other lessons using different reference books and different disciplines. Be creative and have fun.

This unit familiarizes the students with a number of important reference sources. It can be used following Excursion 1 if you want to introduce students to an easier unit than the "Patriot Passage" assignment described in Excursion 3.

For the names of the famous persons and authors, use the enclosed lists or draw up two lists of your own, pulling the names from different volumes so that two students will not need to use the same book. Put these names on sheets of paper and then laminate the paper before cutting it into strips. The students can then draw their own strips from a hat.

164 / Excursion 6: Biography

Name _____

Teacher _____

Date _____ Period _____

Biography Letter Assignment Sheet

Pretend you are a famous author. You are to write a one- to two-page letter addressed from your author, _____ , to a famous person named _____ .

There are four parts to this assignment. Parts 1 and 2 involve doing research and taking notes. Part 3 is writing the letter. Part 4 involves compiling a bibliography.

For Parts 1 and 2, use one or more of the reference books listed on this assignment sheet. Take notes on your "Research Notes" forms using the following note-taking guidelines:

1. Use phrases or key words (no complete sentences)
2. Leave out unimportant words
3. Just write interesting facts that you might use in the letter

Fill in the bibliographic information for each source at the top of each sheet.

PART 1—AUTHOR
1. Where and when your author lived
2. Titles of some of your author's most famous books
3. Short description of your author's style or kinds of books he or she has written
4. One interesting thing or incident concerning your author

   Sources:
   Wilson Author Series
   Authors and Artists for Young Adults
   Contemporary Authors
   Cyclopedia of World Authors
   Major Authors and Illustrators for Children and Young Adults
   Other Author Reference Book

PART 2—FAMOUS PERSON
1. Where and when your famous person lived
2. A description of what he or she did to become famous
3. Two interesting things or incidents concerning your author

From *Cruising Through Research.* © 1998 John D. Volkman. (800) 237-6124.

Fig. 6.1. Photocopy and pass out this assignment sheet to students at the start of the project.

Biography Letter Assignment Sheet / 165

Sources:
Current Biography
Dictionary of American Biography
Encyclopedia of World Biography
Other Biography Reference Book

PART 3—THE LETTER

Using only your completed "Research Notes" forms and your imagination, write the letter. Write the letter like you would to a friend, working the information from your "Research Notes" forms into the letter. Use your creativity to make the letter as interesting as possible. In your letter, do the following:

1. Compare where and when the author and the famous person lived
2. List the titles of a couple of the author's most famous books
3. Give a short description of the author's style or the kind of books he or she has written
4. Tell what the famous person did to become famous
5. Describe and compare the interesting things or incidents concerning the two people
6. Add anything you wish to spice up the letter

PART 4—BIBLIOGRAPHY

Be sure to include a bibliography of your sources at the end of the paper. Get that information from your completed "Research Notes" forms. Here are some examples of the proper bibliographic forms to use:

Kunitz, Stanley J., ed. *American Authors, 1600–1900.* New York: H. W. Wilson, 1938.

May, Hal, ed. *Contemporary Authors.* Detroit: Gale Research, 1983.

Moritz, Charles, ed. *Current Biography Yearbook, 1989.* New York: H. W. Wilson, 1989.

Perkins, Dexter. "W. Wilson." *McGraw-Hill Encyclopedia of World Biography.* New York: McGraw-Hill, 1973.

HAND IN THE FOLLOWING

1. The letter	25 points	_____
2. Completed "Research Notes" forms	20 points	_____
3. Bibliography	5 points	_____
Total	50 points	

From *Cruising Through Research.* © 1998 John D. Volkman. (800) 237-6124.

Famous Authors

Brian Aldiss	Isaac Asimov	Judy Blume
Ray Bradbury	Charlotte Brontë	Emily Brontë
Robert Burns	Beverly Cleary	Stephen Crane
Charles Dickens	George Eliot	William Faulkner
F. Scott Fitzgerald	Paula Fox	Lorraine Hansberry
Nathaniel Hawthorne	S. E. Hinton	Victor Hugo
Shirley Jackson	Madeleine L'Engle	Philip Levine
Jack London	Norma Fox Mazer	Carson McCullers
Gloria Miklowitz	Toni Morrison	Walter Dean Myers
George Orwell	Richard Peck	Edgar Allan Poe
William Saroyan	Gary Soto	John Steinbeck
Todd Strasser	Alfred Tennyson	Leo Tolstoy
Mark Twain	H. G. Wells	Oscar Wilde
Herman Wouk	Richard Wright	Paul Zindel

From *Cruising Through Research*. © 1998 John D. Volkman. (800) 237-6124.

Fig. 6.2. Copy onto colored card stock, laminate, then cut into individual strips (one name per strip). Hand out to students.

Famous Persons

Konrad Adenauer	Susan B. Anthony	Herbert Asquith
Lucille Ball	Mary Bethune	Mary Bethune
Neils Bohr	Luther Burbank	Al Capp
Anthony Comstock	Walter Cronkite	Marie Curie
Eugene Debs	Dorothea Dix	Patty Duke
Thomas Edison	Dian Fossey	Giuseppe Garibaldi
Charles Goodyear	Peter the Great	Wayne Gretzky
Audrey Hepburn	Gregory Hines	Edward Hopper
Janis Joplin	Evel Knievel	Henry Knox
Charles Koop	Martin Luther	Ted Mack
Willie Mays	Joe Montana	Samuel Morse
Louis Pasteur	Walter Reed	Franz Schubert
Claus Spreckels	Bart Starr	Tito
Queen Victoria	Queen Victoria	Eli Whitney

From *Cruising Through Research*, © 1998 John D. Volkman. (800) 237-6124.

Fig. 6.3. Copy onto card stock (different color than fig. 6.2), laminate, then cut into individual strips (one name per strip). Hand out to students.

Excursion 7

Expose a Word

Expose a Word is a fun assignment for giving college prep students practice in doing research. It allows the students to explore many sources and then combine the information learned in a unique manner. The destination for this excursion is gaining knowledge of a variety of reference sources; learning about a particular word is merely the vessel. My ability to adequately enlighten my students about this goal was severely brought into question when, upon completion of the unit, a student told me in an exasperated tone, "Mr. Volkman, I still don't understand why we have to know so much about one word!"

The "Research Notes" form found on page 117 should be used by the students to take their notes. This will aid them in constructing their bibliography and in taking notes properly. For non-book sources, adapt the form to include the necessary bibliographic information.

The words chosen can fall into such categories as abstract words, animals, and nouns. In this example, I include an abstract words list. The sources listed are suggestions; you can easily add other reference books or computer sources depending upon your library and what class is doing the assignment.

170 / Excursion 7: Expose a Word

Name _____

Teacher _____

Date _____ Period _____

Expose a Word Assignment Sheet

WORD CHOSEN: _____

ASSIGNMENT

Look up your assigned word in a variety of sources in the library. For each source you are to use a separate sheet of paper and write down the requested information as well as the complete bibliographic information. From your notes you will then write a paper describing what and how you found out about your word.

SOURCES

1. *UNABRIDGED DICTIONARY.* Look up your word and copy down its first few definitions and its etymology, including the language it is from and its earlier forms. (An explanation of the abbreviations used is found in the front of the dictionary.)

2. *THESAURUS.* Write down some of the synonyms (at least 10 if there are that many).

3. *QUOTATION BOOK.* Use a quotation book such as *Bartlett's Familiar Quotations* or *Home Book of Quotations* to find a quote that contains your word. Write down the quote, who said it, and the book or speech it is from.

4. *BIBLE CONCORDANCE.* Find a verse that contains your word. Look it up in the Bible and copy it down, along with its location in the Bible.

5. *SHAKESPEARE CONCORDANCE.* Find where your word is used in one of Shakespeare's plays. Then find the passage it is taken from in one of the complete works of Shakespeare. Copy down this passage. Be sure to include the name of the play, act, scene, line number, and the name of the character saying the word.

6. *GRANGER'S INDEX TO POETRY OR THE WORLD'S BEST POETRY.* Find a poem that contains your word and copy it down.

7. *INFOTRAC.* Find a magazine article that contains your word. Obtain the magazine and photocopy or print out the article. Then read and summarize it.

8. *NEWSBANK.* Find a newspaper article that contains your word. Make a copy of the article or print it out. Then read and summarize it.

9. *SIRS.* Find an article that contains your word. Make a copy of the article or print it out. Then read and summarize it.

From *Cruising Through Research.* © 1998 John D. Volkman. (800) 237-6124.

Fig. 7.1. Photocopy and pass out to students at the start of the project.

Expose a Word Assignment Sheet / 171

THE PAPER

Describe what you learned, not just about the word but also about the sources and the search itself. You can organize your paper in a variety of ways. Here are some ideas on things to include in it:

1. How your search went and difficulties you encountered in it
2. The most interesting things you learned about the word
3. A description of each source including how to use it and the information you learned from it
4. Which sources were easiest and hardest to use
5. What you learned about doing research
6. What you learned about yourself
7. Your thoughts on this assignment

BIBLIOGRAPHY

Be sure to use the proper form as shown on the sample bibliography sheet and to include all of your sources.

TO BE TURNED IN/GRADING

Eight completed "Research Notes" forms	45 pts.	_____
Rough draft	10 pts.	_____
Bibliography	5 pts.	_____
Written report (final copy)	40 pts.	_____
Total	100 pts.	

From *Cruising Through Research.* © 1998 John D. Volkman. (800) 237-6124.

Expose a Word Word List

ANGER	HEALTH
BEAUTY	HOPE
BRAVE	JOY
DREAM	JUSTICE
ENERGY	KINDNESS
ENVY	KNOWLEDGE
ETERNAL	LOVE
FAITH	MERCY
FEAR	NEIGHBOR
FIGHT	PEACE
FIRE	PRAISE
FREEDOM	REVENGE
FRIENDSHIP	SIN
GOOD	SUCCESS
GRIEF	TIME
HAPPINESS	TRUTH
HATE	WORK

From *Cruising Through Research.* © 1998 John D. Volkman. (800) 237-6124.

Fig. 7.2. Copy onto card stock, laminate, then cut into individual strips (one word per strip). Hand out to students.

Excursion 8
Farewell to Manzanar

This excursion is used as a follow-up activity to the reading of *Farewell to Manzanar* by Jeanne Houston. Similar lessons can be constructed to help students research the background of other books. I include pictures from books on the internment on the assignment sheet. You can do the same by finding appropriate pictures and either scanning or photocopying them onto your student handouts. The handout presented in figure 8.1 can be given to teachers who check out the class sets of the book. Similar sheets can be created for other books that your classes read. Figure 8.2 is the assignment sheet to be given to students.

174 / Excursion 8: Farewell to Manzanar

Ideas for Teachers Introducing This Unit

1. The day before introducing the book, *Farewell to Manzanar*, tell the students that for homework, they are to think or write about the following: They have been told that they have 24 hours to leave their home and move to a new location. They can only pack what will fit in two suitcases. What will they pack and why?

2. Clarify the three reasons why the Japanese internment was able to take place: mass hysteria, poor leadership, and racism, all stirred up by the media.

3. Note that only the United States has ever had the wherewithal to admit a mistake of this type and attempt to make restitution. In other instances (e.g., Germany's treatment of the Jews and Turkey's treatment of the Armenians), the countries involved basically ignored or even denied the accusations made against them.

4. See the librarian to update the assignment and bibliography, and to sign up your class for library time.

5. The library has the excellent video *Gaman: The Internment Remembered*, which was made by survivors of the internment. It is an excellent follow-up to the book and is about 30 minutes long.

6. Related young-adult fiction books showing prejudice against classes of people which have ideas that can be used in your class include:

The Wave by Todd Strasser. New York: Dell, 1981.

The War Between the Classes by Gloria D. Miklowitz. New York: Dell, 1986.

The first three ideas are from a conversation I had with Jeanne Houston at the California School Library Association conference in November 1995.

From *Cruising Through Research.* © 1998 John D. Volkman. (800) 237-6124.

Fig. 8.1. Distribute to teachers who check out the class sets of books.

Name _____

Teacher _____

Date _____ Period _____

Farewell to Manzanar Assignment Sheet

In conjunction with the reading of *Farewell to Manzanar* each student will write a short research paper on an aspect of the Japanese-American internment during World War II.

ASSIGNMENT
1. Your paper is to be a minimum of three double-spaced, typed pages.
2. Choose one of the following topics:
   - The *Panay* incident
   - Japanese soldiers in Europe
   - Japanese Exclusion Order 9066
   - Roosevelt's prior knowledge of the Pearl Harbor attack
   - Hiroshima
   - Japanese-American involvement prior to World War II
   - Guadalcanal
   - Midway Island
   - President Reagan's order to give $20,000 in restitution to internees
   - The Manzanar Camp in Owens Valley, California
   - U.S. Bureau of Immigration and Naturalization—emphasis on Japanese naturalization rights
   - California's Alien Land Bill preventing Japanese ownership of land in California
   - Kamikaze pilots
   - Supreme Court cases ruling the internment illegal

TURN IN
1. Title page
2. Typed report
3. "Research Notes" forms/photocopies
4. Rough draft
5. Bibliography

From *Cruising Through Research*. © 1998 John D. Volkman. (800) 237-6124.

Fig. 8.2. Photocopy and pass out to students at the start of the project.

MINIMUM RESOURCE REQUIREMENTS
1. Four sources (books or periodicals)
2. Ten "Research Notes" forms/photocopies

GRADING

"Research Notes" forms/photocopies	20 pts.	_____
Rough draft	20 pts.	_____
Written report (final copy)	50 pts.	_____
Bibliography/minimum sources	10 pts.	_____
Total	100 pts.	

SOURCES
1. Reference Books

    American Heritage History of U.S.

    Dictionary of American History

    Encyclopedia of the American Constitution

    The Marshall Cavendish Illustrated Encyclopedia of World War II

    Other Reference Books on WWII

2. Non-Fiction Section

    Books on World War II

    Books on American concentration camps

    Books on U.S. history

3. Computers

    Facts on File, Infotrac, or Newsbank (articles on *recent* events, found under such categories as "Restitution")

Excursion 9
Endangered Species

The cargo for this excursion follows the basic pattern set out in "Before You Sail" and needs little introduction. It has been used not only in science classes, but in English classes as a follow-up to the reading of *Never Cry Wolf* by Farley Mowat. Two sources of the names of endangered animals are the *Endangered Wildlife of the World* set and the list at the back of the last volume of *The Marshall Cavendish International Wildlife Encyclopedia*.

178 / Excursion 9: Endangered Species

Name _____

Teacher _____

Date _____ Period _____

Endangered Species Assignment Sheet

YOUR SPECIES: _____

DUE DATE: _____

ASSIGNMENT

1. You are to write a three to four page research report on an endangered species.
2. You are to address the following subjects:
    a. Common name and scientific name of your animal
    b. Description
        1) Physical description, including size and color.
        2) Niche/job—placement in the food chain, the importance of this organism's contribution to the ecology, and how other organisms are affected by this organism's declining numbers
        3) Life history/lifestyle—life span, community, mating, care of young
        4) Intriguing facts or peculiarities
    c. Distribution and habitat. *Distribution* refers to where it is found; *habitat* refers to the kind of environment it requires or prefers. Include migration, if it applies.
    d. Reason for decline: Why is this organism disappearing?
    e. Protective measures: What is being done to preserve this species?

TURN IN

1. Cover
2. Typed report
3. Pictures of your animal and its habitat
4. All "Research Notes" forms and photocopies

From *Cruising Through Research*. © 1998 John D. Volkman. (800) 237-6124.

Fig. 9.1. Photocopy and pass out to student at the start of the project.

Endangered Species Assignment Sheet / 179

MINIMUM RESOURCE REQUIREMENTS

1. One *Endangered Wildlife of the World* article
2. Two other reference books
3. One other book
4. One periodical article

GRADING

"Research Notes" forms/photocopies	20 pts.	_____
Pictures	10 pts.	_____
Rough draft	10 pts.	_____
Written report (final copy)	30 pts.	_____
Bibliography/minimum sources	5 pts.	_____
Total	75 pts.	

From *Cruising Through Research.* © 1998 John D. Volkman. (800) 237-6124.

ENDANGERED SPECIES—SOURCES

1. Start with the REFERENCE (R) BOOKS in the 591-599 section.

2. Use the computer card catalog to look-up topics such as:
RARE ANIMALS
ENDANGERED SPECIES
ANIMALS
Specific name of your animal
(There are also many books on animals in the 591-599 section of the regular shelves.)

3. Use periodical sources from the computer network about your animal:
Newsbank (newspapers)
TOM/Infotrac (magazines)

Excursion 10
Foreign Languages, Foreign Countries

These activities can be used either in foreign language classes, social studies classes, or geography classes. I have used Hispanic countries for the examples, but of course you can substitute other languages, countries, or cultures.

"Latin American Countries" is an introductory unit designed to move the students beyond encyclopedias and to teach them about the more specific reference works available in the library (see fig. 10.1).

"Traveling in an Hispanic Country" is for advanced students because it requires more sophisticated research and presentation skills. Typically, it is done by our second- and third-year Spanish classes (see fig. 10.2).

"Biography of an Hispanic Person, Past or Present" can be adapted for any kind of a biography report. It includes information on how to direct the students to sources by use of a written list (see fig. 10.3). It is always a good idea to have a list of persons from which the students can either choose or draw names; such a list is included here (see fig. 10.4).

182 / Excursion 10: Foreign Languages, Foreign Countries

Name _____

Teacher _____

Date _____ Period _____

Latin American Countries Assignment Sheet

COUNTRY: _____

For each question write your answer, the name of your source, and the page number on which you found the answer. You must use at least three different sources for your answers.

1. Population of country: _____
   Source: _____ Page: _____

2. Type of Government: _____
   Source: _____ Page: _____

3. Language: _____
   Source: _____ Page: _____

4. Weather/Climate: _____
   _____
   Source: _____ Page: _____

5. The main industries: _____
   _____
   _____
   Source: _____ Page: _____

From *Cruising Through Research.* © 1998 John D. Volkman. (800) 237-6124.

Fig. 10.1. Photocopy and pass out to students at the start of the project.

Latin American Countries Assignment Sheet / 183

6. Photocopy a map of your country from an atlas; color it and circle the capital of the country.

   Source: _____ Page: _____

7. Draw and color your country's flag on the back of this paper.

   Source: _____ Page: _____

SOURCES:
Atlases
Almanac
Countries of the World/Background Notes
Encyclopedia of the Third World
Encyclopedia of World Geography
Lands and Peoples
Worldmark Encyclopedia of Nations

Name _____

Teacher _____

Date _____ Period _____

Traveling in an Hispanic Country

Due to your demonstrated mastery of Spanish and extensive knowledge of the country of _____, you have been hired to give an oral presentation to a group of people planning to travel to that country.

TOPICS TO BE ADDRESSED IN YOUR PRESENTATION
1. Facts that travelers need to know, such as
   a. Transportation
   b. Accommodations
   c. Health concerns
   d. Monetary exchange
2. Climate
3. Capital
4. Other cities, historical places, scenic places, national parks and monuments
5. Festivals or holidays
6. Recreational, sports, or cultural events
7. Typical foods or specialties
8. Important industries or crafts

YOUR PRESENTATION ALSO WILL INCLUDE VISUALS ON A POSTER BOARD
1. Map showing areas you are describing (Use an atlas or computer)
2. Pictures, brochures, flag, artwork

From *Cruising Through Research*. © 1998 John D. Volkman. (800) 237-6124.

Fig. 10.2. Photocopy and pass out to students at the start of the project.

RESEARCH REQUIREMENTS
At least four resources must be used from these types of sources:
1. Reference books
2. Travel agencies
3. Computer
4. Embassy/consulate offices

GRADING
1. Oral presentation	50 pts.	_____
2. Notes	15 pts.	_____
3. Poster board with visuals	15 pts.	_____
4. Outline (not written report)	10 pts.	_____
5. Bibliography	10 pts.	_____
Total	100 pts.	

SPANISH-SPEAKING COUNTRIES—SOURCES

1. Start with reference books such as the following:
   Almanacs (for most current information and statistics)
   Background Notes
   Cities of the World (4 volumes)
   Countries of the World (2 volumes)
   Encyclopedia of the Third World (3 volumes)
   The Illustrated Encyclopedia of Mankind (21 volumes)
   Lands and People (6 volumes)
   Worldmark Encyclopedia of Nations (5 volumes)

2. Look for magazine articles and pictures using:
   Infotrac
   National Geographic Index
   SIRS Government Reporter (includes background notes)

3. Look up the name of the country in the computer or card catalog.

4. If available, access PC Globe (a computer program to locate maps, statistics, and anthems)

Name _____

Teacher _____

Date _____ Period _____

Biography of an Hispanic Person, Past or Present

PERSON: _____

ASSIGNMENT

You are going to present an oral report to the class about a notable Hispanic person. The oral report can be presented with a partner who has researched a different person than you. The two of you will carry on a dialogue comparing and contrasting your persons. Your report should contain the following information about your person:

1. Facts
    a. When born
    b. Where born
    c. When died
2. Family
    a. Information about parents, brothers, sisters
    b. Where raised
3. Education and training
4. Road to fame
5. Contributions to Hispanic culture, achievements
6. Personality traits
7. Disappointments in life or career
8. Other people's opinion of this person
9. Influence on society
10. Your personal opinion and analysis

Your presentation also will include visuals such as pictures, maps, and drawings on a poster board.

From *Cruising Through Research*. © 1998 John D. Volkman. (800) 237-6124.

Fig. 10.3. Photocopy and pass out to student at the start of the project.

188 / Excursion 10: Foreign Languages, Foreign Countries

RESEARCH REQUIREMENTS
At least four resources must be used from these types of sources:
1. Reference books
2. Computer card catalog
3. Computer databases

GRADING
1. Oral presentation   50 pts.   _____
2. Notes   15 pts.   _____
3. Poster board with visuals   15 pts.   _____
4. Outline (not written report)   10 pts.   _____
5. Bibliography   10 pts.   _____
Total   100 pts.

SOURCES
1. Start with the following reference books.
   American Decades
   Current Biography (Use index to see which year applies)
   Extraordinary Hispanic Americans
   Hispanic Almanac
   Hispanic American Almanac
   Hispanic American Biography (2 volumes)
   Hispanic Writers
   Latino Experience
   Latino Encyclopedia (6 volumes)
   McGraw-Hill Encyclopedia of World Biography (12 volumes)
   Mexican Portraits
   Notable Hispanic American Women

2. Use the card catalog program in the computer to look under the last name of your person to see if there is a biography of that person.

3. If your subject falls into a specific category, you can check specialized reference or regular books in categories such as the following:

364.9	Crime and Criminals	703	Art
791.43	Movies	791.45	Television
784	Rock music (You may have to ask at the information desk for some of these books)	920.5	Scientists
796	Sports	920.8	Authors

From *Cruising Through Research*. © 1998 John D. Volkman. (800) 237-6124.

Los Hispanos Famosos

(Famous Hispanics)

Maria Conchita Alonso	Desi Arnaz
Joan Baez	Seve Ballesteros
Manuel Benitez ("El Cordobes")	Simon Bolivar
Jose Canseco	Rod Carew
Juan (King) Carlos I	Pablo Casals
Fidel Castro	Miguel de Cervantes
César Chavez	Julio "Cesar" Chavez
Roberto Clemente	Salvador Dalí
Oscar de la Hoya	Rodrigo de Vicar ("El Cid")
Placido Domingo	Hector Elizondo
Gloria Esteban	Emilio Estevez
Jose Feliciano	Francisco Franco
Daisy Fuentes	Andy Garcia
Amalia Hernandez	Carolina Herrera
Dolores Huerta	Julio Iglesias
Raul Julia	Nancy Lopez
Sonia Manzano	Diego Maradona
Juan Marichal	Rita Moreno

List continues on page 190.

From *Cruising Through Research.* © 1998 John D. Volkman. (800) 237-6124.

Fig. 10.4. Photocopy onto card stock, laminate, and cut into individual author names. Hand out to students.

Edward James Olmos
Pio Pico
Selena Quintanilla-Perez
Geraldo Rivera
Paul M. Rodriguez
Linda Ronstadt
Arantxa Sanchez-Vicario
Andres Segovia
Juan Serrano
Jimmy Smits
Gregorio Tamayo
Rudy Trevino
Luis Valdez
Guillermo Vilas

Pablo Picasso
Jim Plunkett
Diego Rivera
Chi Chi Rodriguez
Rich Rodriguez
Gabriela Sabatini
Carlos Santana
Junipero Serra
Charlie Sheen
Gary Soto
Lee Trevino
Richie Valens
Fernando Valenzuela

Excursion 11
Astronomy

This assignment can be used as a prototype for other science projects. It is similar in format to the previous assignments, but it does differ in some respects because it reflects not just my work as a librarian but also the ideas of the science teacher doing the project. One of the real joys of being a librarian is developing lessons cooperatively with the classroom teachers. Use the ideas and requirements they specify for their unit, but do it so that it incorporates the basic guidelines of "Before You Set Sail" (pp. xiii-xv).

Students may choose their own topics on a first-come, first-served basis. Have a sign-up sheet so that you can keep track of which topics are taken.

With the blank space available on the assignment sheet, I like to include pictures of such things as the solar system, a space ship, or an astronomer. I always like to include graphics, either photocopies or computer-generated pictures, to add a little zip to the written words. Keep this idea in mind when constructing units, and have some fun with illustrative material.

192 / Excursion 11: Astronomy

Name _____

Teacher _____

Date _____ Period _____

Astronomy Project

TOPIC _____

ASSIGNMENT

1. This assignment will be done in pairs. You and your partner are to make an oral presentation on a topic in astronomy. Most of the work must be completed outside of class. We will, however, spend some class time in the library. Use that time wisely.

2. Only one partnership per class may work on a particular topic. However, other groups from other classes may be working on the same topic you have. Therefore, it would be wise to do your library research right away. If you wait until the last minute, do not expect to find as much material.

ORAL PRESENTATION

1. You and your partner must both participate.

2. Present seven to ten minutes of information about your topic, reflecting your research.

3. Use visuals such as pictures, models, drawings, and videotape.

OUTLINE

1. You are to turn in a three to four page outline of the information you find on your project.

2. The outline must be typed or written in ink on one side of the paper only.

BIBLIOGRAPHY

1. In the bibliography, you are to cite the sources or references you have used.

2. You must use proper form.

From *Cruising Through Research.* © 1998 John D. Volkman. (800) 237-6124.

Fig. 11.1. Photocopy and pass out to students at the start of the project.

GRADING

1. Oral presentation	45 pts.	_____
2. "Research Notes" forms	15 pts.	_____
3. Visuals	15 pts.	_____
4. Outline (not written report)	15 pts.	_____
5. Bibliography	10 pts.	_____
Total	100 pts.	

MINIMUM RESOURCE REQUIREMENTS

The information on your topic must come from at least three sources selected from the following options:

1. Book (Astronomy - 523, Space Travel - 629.4)
2. Encyclopedia
3. Periodical (magazine or newspaper article, located using library computers)
4. TV program
5. Internet
6. Computer programs you have at home
7. Experts in the field

TOPICS

Asteroid belt	Kepler	Radio telescopes
Astronauts	Mars	Satellites
Binary stars	Mercury	Saturn
Black holes	Meteors	Space shuttles
Challenger	Milky Way	Space stations
Comets	Moon	Supernova
Constellations	Navigation (North Star)	UFOs
Copernicus	Nebula	Uranus
Galaxies	Newton	Variable star
Galileo	Pluto	Venus
Halley's comet	Pulsars	Viking missions
Jupiter	Quasars	White dwarfs

From *Cruising Through Research*. © 1998 John D. Volkman. (800) 237-6124.

Excursion 12
Vietnam

Vietnam Instructions

For those of us who were teenagers during the '60s, there have now been more years between the Vietnam War and now than there were between World War II and when we were in high school. Remember how *we* thought World War II was ancient history? Since the Vietnam War and the '60s have so greatly affected what American society is today, I wanted the students to get a feel for what that era was like through a variety of experiences.

In this extensive unit, students learn about the Vietnam War by spending about 30 minutes at each of six stations set up around the library. The stations include a map assignment, a research assignment, listening to music of the era, reading Vietnam veterans' poetry, and reading and drawing graphics for editorials and letters sent home from Vietnam soldiers.

This unit is done by the juniors in our United States history classes. These students have been in the library for many research projects including the World War II unit. Therefore, they are familiar with library research but will now get some new experiences in the library.

Students do a great job on this unit and have a lot of fun doing it. They especially love to listen to the songs. They also get a feel for what it was like to be away from home in a foreign land, fighting to stay alive. They also interact with each other as they draw their graphics. It is amazing to see how even the least-talented artists can still come up with a thoughtful drawing.

196 / Excursion 12: Vietnam

Before the project is assigned, there are a number of things the librarians or teacher must do:

1. Have a large number of colored pencils (Station 1).
2. Record a tape of Vietnam era songs (Station 3).
3. Find, photocopy, and laminate Vietnam veterans' poetry selections (Station 4).
4. Find, photocopy, and laminate editorials (Station 5).
5. Find, photocopy, and laminate soldiers' letters (Station 6).
6. Photocopy figures 12.1 through 12.5 and 12.7 through 12.8 so that there are enough for one per student.

Station 1

Students are given an instruction sheet (fig. 12.2) telling them what to label and a blank map of Southeast Asia (fig. 12.3). Have at this station the appropriate atlases and other reference books to help them in their task. Use the books listed on the assignment sheet or others you may have. Also have colored pencils available for the students to use.

Station 2

Set up a table with all available books on Vietnam on it to help students easily find their topics. The assignment (see fig. 12.4) is done in groups of four with each student researching five topics. The five topic summaries are then photocopied and given to each of the other three members of the group. Before coming to the library, students should be divided into research teams of four. If there is an odd number of students, use one group of five (four topics per person instead of five). They do not need to work together at the station but will exchange research answers after the work is done.

Station 3

Record some representative songs dealing with the Vietnam War. Use the titles and questions listed in figure 12.5 or have fun recording your own selections. Some other possible songs are listed in figure 12.6. It is helpful to time the songs and put in the length of the selection after the name of each song. Songs may be shortened so that you can get more on the tape; you should have about 25 minutes worth of music. Students listen to the tape and fill in the answers as they listen. Also, you might want to photocopy pictures of the artists and put them on posterboard.

Station 4

Here, the students read poems written by Vietnam veterans and write their reactions to and thoughts about them (see fig. 12.7). A good source for poems is *Winning Hearts and Minds: War Poems by Vietnam Veterans*, edited by Larry Rottmann (New York: McGraw-Hill, 1972).

Station 5

Find about seven or eight editorials or primary source articles. You might want to use articles from *The Annals of America* (Chicago: Encyclopaedia Britannica, 1968), articles from magazines published at that time, and "Primary Sources" from Teachers' Curriculum Institute (2465 Latham, Suite 100, Mountain View, CA 94040. Phone 800-497-6138). Photocopy three copies (two for each pair and one extra) of the editorials and laminate them. The students work together in pairs, each reading the article and then drawing one graphic (see fig. 12.8). They photocopy or redraw the graphic so that each of them can have one for their notebook. Have seven or eight laminated copies of the students' instructions, colored pencils, and plain white paper available at this station.

Station 6

The students' instructions for the letters are the same as those for the editorials (see fig. 12.8). Use the letters from the book *Dear America: Letters Home from Vietnam*, edited by Bernard Edelman (New York: Norton, 1985). There are eight chapters in the book. For each sheet photocopy the introduction to the chapter and then a few representative letters. Photocopy three copies (two for each pair and one extra) of each sheet and laminate them. Have seven or eight laminated copies of the students' instructions, colored pencils, and plain white paper available at this station.

Teacher Directions for Vietnam Project

Folders

Each student needs a folder with pockets in which to put all of the papers from the assignment. Ten extra points are awarded if the folder is turned in before the first day in the library. The teacher can stamp the folder to show that it was turned in early and then return it to the student. Ten points are subtracted if no folder is turned in with the notebook.

Stations

The day before coming to the library, divide the class into six groups: A B C D E F.

The students will stay in these groups all three days and go to the stations as shown below:

Day 1:	1 2	3 4	5 6
	A B	C D	E F
Day 2:	1 2	3 4	5 6
	C D	E F	A B
Day 3:	1 2	3 4	5 6
	E F	A B	C D

Flip-flop the groups halfway through period (after about 25 minutes).

Vietnam Notebook Cover Sheet / 199

Name _____

Teacher _____

Date _____ Period _____

Vietnam Notebook Cover Sheet

Your notebook will include the following, clearly labeled, in the order given.

Your Points	Possible Points		
_____	10	**Station 1:**	**Map Activity** • Complete map activity
_____	40	**Station 2:**	**Research Assignment** • Typed copies of all 20 topics completed by your group in numerical order by section
_____	10	**Station 3:**	**Music** • Listen to tape of popular music of the era • Complete student assignment sheet
_____	15	**Station 4:**	**Poetry** • Read poems written by former soldiers • Complete student assignment sheet
_____	15	**Station 5:**	**Editorials and Commentaries** • Read and respond to primary source/editorial/commentary from Vietnam era • Complete notes and graphic of major ideas with a partner
_____	10	**Station 6:**	**Letters Home** • Read and react to letters written home by Vietnam soldiers • Complete notes and graphic of major ideas with a partner
_____	100	**Total Points**	
_____		**Your Grade**	

From *Cruising Through Research*. © 1998 John D. Volkman. (800) 237-6124.

Fig. 12.1. Photocopy and pass out to students at the start of the project.

200 / Excursion 12: Vietnam

Name _____

Teacher _____

Date _____ Period _____

Station 1—Map Activity Sheet

1. Label the following countries and color each a different color:
   - Laos
   - Thailand
   - Cambodia
   - North Vietnam
   - South Vietnam
   - China

2. Label the following bodies of water:
   - South China Sea
   - Gulf of Tonkin
   - Mekong Delta

3. Draw and label the following:
   - Ho Chi Minh Trail
   - DMZ (the Demilitarized Zone, 17th parallel)

4. Locate on your map with a dot and label the following cities:
   - Hanoi
   - Da Nang
   - Haiphong
   - Saigon
   - Phnom Penh
   - Hue
   - Khe Sanh
   - My Lai
   - Dien Bien Phu

5. What was the capital of North Vietnam? _____

6. What was the capital of South Vietnam? _____

RESOURCES:
Atlas of Battles (pp. 148–149)
American Heritage Pictorial Atlas of U.S. History (pp. 322–323)
Atlas of American Wars (pp. 149, 151)
War in Peace, Volume 5 (p. 952)
The Vietnam War (p. 31)

Regular world atlases such as Hammond, Rand McNally, Goode. (Refer to index.)

From *Cruising Through Research.* © 1998 John D. Volkman. (800) 237-6124.

Fig. 12.2. Photocopy and pass out to students at the start of the project.

Station 1—Map Activity Sheet / 201

Name _____

Teacher _____

Date _____ Period _____

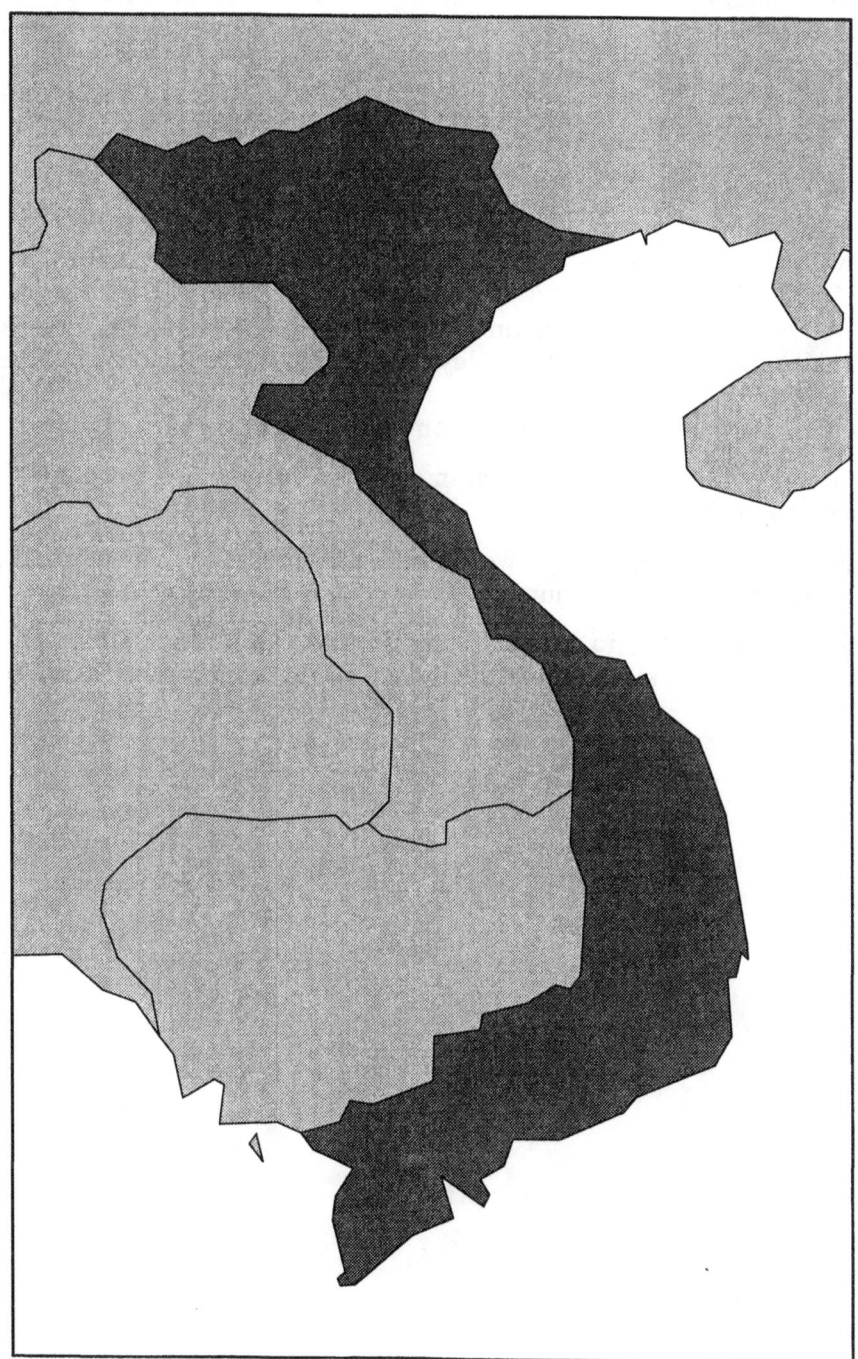

From *Cruising Through Research.* © 1998 John D. Volkman. (800) 237-6124.

Fig. 12 3. Photocopy and pass out to students at the start of the project.

Station 2—Vietnam Topics

Section 1
1. Pentagon Papers
2. Diem Assassination
3. Gulf of Tonkin
4. Buddhist Protest
5. Tet Offensive

Section 2
6. Cambodia
7. War Powers Act
8. Agent Orange/Napalm
9. Draft Dodgers/Amnesty Program
10. My Lai Massacre/Lt. William Calley

Section 3
11. Fall of Saigon
12. Secret War in Laos
13. POWs/MIAs
14. Paris Peace Talks
15. Kent State

Section 4
16. Vietnam War Memorial
17. Vietnamization
18. Peace With Honor
19. Dissent and Protest
20. Gulf of Tonkin Resolution

Each person in the group of four is responsible for one section of five topics.

1. For each topic, write a 1/2 page or more description or summary. Include the number of each topic.

2. All summaries must be typed or word processed. Print or photocopy all summaries for each member of your group.

3. Each student will turn in all 20 topics in the completed folder. Be sure each section of 5 topics has the name of the group member who did them on it.

From *Cruising Through Research*. © 1998 John D. Volkman. (800) 237-6124.

Fig. 12.4. Photocopy and pass out to students at the start of the project.

Name _____

Teacher _____

Date _____ Period _____

Station 3—Vietnam Era Songs

Read each question. Listen to the recording. Write down your answers.

1. "War"—Edwin Starr originally released this hit in 1969. More black soldiers fought in Vietnam than any other American group, so it seems appropriate that the first anti-war protest song to reach number one was by a black artist on a black label. Bruce Springsteen performed a memorable cover version of it at a concert in 1985.
   What is war good for?

2. "Blowin' in the Wind"—Bob Dylan wrote and performed this song, but the most popular and largest-selling version was by Peter, Paul, and Mary.
   Dylan is asking questions that people have asked since the beginning of time. What does the refrain "blowin' in the wind" mean?

3. "Ohio"—Crosby, Stills, Nash, and Young recorded this song about the 1970 Kent State protest. Kent State University in Ohio was the site of student demonstrations which included the burning down of the ROTC building. National Guard troops were sent in to stop the violence, and four students were shot and killed.
   Who were the "tin soldiers," and who was Nixon?

From *Cruising Through Research.* © 1998 John D. Volkman. (800) 237-6124.

Fig. 12.5. Photocopy and pass out to students at the start of the project.

204 / Excursion 12: Vietnam

4. "For What It's Worth"—Buffalo Springfield recorded this song written by group member, Stephen Stills, when he saw a man carrying a large revolver on a street in Los Angeles. His fears of death and guns reflected in this song were quickly adopted as an anthem by the war protest movement.

   What might the lines in this song mean in relation to what was happening with the war protest, the draft, and the killing in the Vietnam War?

5. "Give Peace a Chance"—John Lennon and his wife, Yoko Ono, recorded this song while staging a "bed-in" (they stayed in bed for a week) for peace in Toronto in 1969.

   What was the name of the group John Lennon used to be in?

6. "Ballad of the Green Berets"—Staff Sergeant Barry Sadler wrote and performed this Grammy award-winning, number-one song in 1966 when the majority of Americans still supported the war. His song is about the elite soldiers who were called on to perform the toughest assignments in Vietnam.

   As you hear the words of this song, what are your reactions?

7. "Eve of Destruction"—In this song, Barry McGuire expresses powerful antiwar sentiments that set off immediate controversy. It was banned by many U.S. radio stations but still turned gold and topped the United States recording chart in 1965.

   What are some antiwar themes mentioned in the song?

War Protest Songs

There are many Vietnam War protest songs. In addition to the ones listed in figure 12.5, here are some other titles that you might be able to find and use:

"Where Have All the Flowers Gone?"—Kingston Trio or Pete Seger

"Universal Soldier"—Donovan

"I Feel Like I'm Fixin' to Die Rag"—Country Joe McDonald and the Fish

"Sky Pilot"—Eric Burdon

"People Got to Be Free"—The Rascals

"With God on Our Side"—Manfred Mann

"Volunteers"—Jefferson Airplane

From *Cruising Through Research*. © 1998 John D. Volkman. (800) 237-6124

Fig. 12.6. Choose some of these songs to record on the Vietnam Era songs tape that you create for Station 3.

206 / Excursion 12: Vietnam

Name _____

Teacher _____

Date _____ Period _____

Station 4—Vietnam Poetry

Read each of the following poems. Write a sentence or two on what you think the poem means or what reactions you felt.

1. "Sounds of War"—Stanley Brownstein

2. "Gut Catcher"—Stan Platke

3. "The Longest War"—Jan Barry

4. "Viet Nam–February 1967"—W. D. Ehrhart

5. "Vietnam"—Robert C. Hahn

6. "Chewing Gum & Soap"—Serigo

7. "Hue City"—Serigo

8. "A Sunday Afternoon Pickup Game"—Larry Rottmann

From *Cruising Through Research.* © 1998 John D. Volkman. (800) 237-6124.

Fig. 12.7. Photocopy and pass out to student at the start of the project.

Stations 5 and 6— Vietnam Editorial and Commentary, Letters Home Graphics

1. Assignment is done in pairs.
2. Each pair gets one set of the editorial or letter.
3. Read the editorial or letter.
4. Take notes or write down your general impressions.
5. Create a single page graphic to illustrate your impressions.

REQUIREMENTS FOR GRAPHIC

1. A graphic should use color, symbols, and words.
2. You may use short and meaningful quotations from the selection. Choose phrases that communicate an idea and are not long.
3. Give your graphic a title.

From *Cruising Through Research.* © 1998 John D. Volkman. (800) 237-6124.

Fig. 12.8. Photocopy and laminate seven or eight copies for use at Station 5 and seven or eight copies for use at Station 6.

www.ingramcontent.com/pod-product-compliance
Lightning Source LLC
Chambersburg PA
CBHW080936300426
44115CB00017B/2847